MESSAGES GIVEN TO THE WORKING SAINTS

Witness Lee

Living Stream Ministry
Anaheim, CA • www.lsm.org

© 1989 Living Stream Ministry

All rights reserved. No part of this work may be reproduced or transmitted in any form or by any means—graphic, electronic, or mechanical, including photocopying, recording, or information storage and retrieval systems—without written permission from the publisher.

First Edition, November 1989.

ISBN 978-0-87083-480-6

Published by

Living Stream Ministry
2431 W. La Palma Ave., Anaheim, CA 92801 U.S.A.
P. O. Box 2121, Anaheim, CA 92814 U.S.A.

Printed in India

10 11 12 13 14 15 / 11 10 9 8 7 6 5

CONTENTS

Title	Page
Preface	5
1 The Goal of the God-ordained Way—Building Up the Body of Christ	7
2 The Practical Steps of God's Ordained Way	15
3 The Divine Power of God and the Precious Promises of the Lord	25
4 The Miraculously Normal Living in the New Way	37
5 The Father's Strengthening and Christ's Making Home	49
6 The Relationship between the Working Saints and the New Way in the Lord's Recovery	59
7 Give Up the World Christ to Obtain	69
8 A Normal Life and Service	85

PREFACE

This book is composed of messages given by Brother Witness Lee in Taipei, Taiwan in April, May, and June of 1988.

CHAPTER ONE

THE GOAL OF THE GOD-ORDAINED WAY—BUILDING UP THE BODY OF CHRIST

Scripture Reading: Eph. 4:8-16

OUTLINE

I. Building up the Body being different from building up a congregation:
   A. Building up a congregation being organizational.
   B. Building up the Body being organic.
II. Building up the organic Body of Christ:
   A. Needing Christ as the Head—vv. 8-11:
     1. Having perfected the gifted ones through overcoming and ascension.
     2. Having given the gifted ones to His Body.
   B. Needing the gifted ones—vv. 11-12:
     1. Having apostles, prophets, evangelists, and shepherds and teachers.
     2. For the perfecting of the saints to be able to do the work of ministry, the building up of the Body of Christ.
   C. Needing the perfected members—vv. 15-16:
     1. Holding to truth in love.
     2. Growing into the Head, Christ, in all things.
     3. Being joined and knit together:
       a. Through every joint of the supply.
       b. According to the operation in measure of each one part.
     4. Causing the growth of the Body.
     5. Building up the Body in love.

Thank the Lord for giving us this conference in these two evenings. I consider this very important, and I treasure it very much. In these two meetings, our burden is to help the brothers and sisters to see in a brief way the goal of God's ordained way and the way to practice it. For this, we need to speak for the Lord according to the high standard of the Bible. I hope that every brother and sister will exercise his spirit and his sound mind to understand and receive this word. I also look to the Lord's grace from above that I can present this new way clearly and completely.

First of all, we need to know that the God-ordained way, which is the new way that we have been talking about in the past three years, is an ancient way in the Bible. The way that the apostles brought in two thousand years ago and the way that the early church took was this way. However, due to her degradation, the church gradually fell into the world, deviated from the revelation in the Bible, and took an old way about which we have spoken. After receiving light in the Bible before the Lord, we, by the Lord's grace, are willing to recover the lost scriptural way. Therefore, in the Lord's recovery, this has become a new way. Actually, this new way which we are recovering is the ancient way which was practiced by the church two thousand years ago. This is the way ordained by God according to His eternal purpose.

You may say that this way, from the beginning to the end, was revealed to us in the New Testament little by little in a very clear way. However, due to the fact that there is nothing of this new way in our natural concept, we could not discover it from our reading. When we read the Bible, mostly we have deeper impressions concerning the things which are already within us; hence, we echo to them immediately upon reading. However, concerning those profound things within God's heart, we have no idea, and we cannot understand even after much reading. Let us take Ephesians 4:8-16 as an example. There are many points there which are profound; we can read them, yet we have no way to understand. We find it difficult to understand such a profound matter. We need to look to the Lord to grant us revelation and light that we may see the profound things of God in this portion of the Word.

This portion of the Word primarily talks about the building up of the Body of Christ, which is the goal of the God-ordained way. When we first mentioned the new way, it seemed that the impression we gave the brothers and sisters was that the goal of the new way was door-knocking. But I have to say that preaching the gospel by door-knocking is not the goal of the new way. Even all the home meetings, group meetings, or district meetings are not the goal of the new way. The goal of the new way is the building up of the Body of Christ. Then why do we still have to preach the gospel by door-knocking? It is because the building up of the Body of Christ requires material. In order to obtain the material, we have to preach the gospel. The reason we go out to knock on doors is for preaching the gospel, leading people to be regenerated, to be saved, and to become material for the building up of the Body of Christ. The home meetings are for the perfecting of the newly saved ones, for leading them to function in the meetings. A further step is to have group meetings to group the saints together that they may have a place to have mutual fellowship, to be knit together, to care for one another, and to be built up with each other. Then we arrive at the district meeting where we help people to enter more into the church life, to function organically in the meetings, and to speak to and supply one another for mutual building up. All these added together are for the building up of the Body of Christ.

THE BUILDING UP OF THE BODY BEING DIFFERENT FROM BUILDING UP A CONGREGATION

Every one of us has a body, which is our physical body. Christ also has a Body, which is His Church. Apparently our body is an organization organized by many members grouped together. However, it is not quite the same as a table made of many pieces of wood. The table is a lifeless organization; the body is an organism of life. As long as something is a part of the body, regardless of whether it is big or small, it has the organic feeling and function. Similarly, the Body of Christ, the church, is not an organization, but an organism. Therefore, our building up of the church of Christ is not building up a congregation, an organization, or a social group. The old way of tradition in Christianity does not pay attention to the

Body of Christ, but only to the outward organization. That old way encourages people to join a religion. Once they have joined the religion, they became a member of that group. Then everyone comes together to elect each other. They form a board of directors, a committee, and elect different kinds of committee members. This is a congregation, not the Body of Christ. The Body of Christ is a group of people who have repented, believed, and received Jesus as their Savior and life. They have been regenerated in their spirit, and they have the Holy Spirit moving and filling them within to cause them to be transformed, to grow, and to become organic members.

Tonight I am standing here. If I did not have an organic body to coordinate with my life, then this living person of mine would have no way to be expressed. The Lord Jesus is a great One who fills all; He needs a great organism to express Him. However, until today, He still has not obtained this great organism which is the proper church. We have been in the Lord's recovery for many decades, and the Lord's recovery has spread to the six continents having more than eleven hundred local churches. However, the percentage that we are organic is not that much; we are still lacking the organic expression of the life functions. Our situation is still mostly one of organization. This is altogether the result of the old way. Therefore, there is an extremely great need for us to walk from the old way to the new way that has been given to us by the Lord in order to develop the organic functions of the members so that the Lord may have an organic Body.

BUILDING UP THE ORGANIC BODY OF CHRIST

Needing Christ as the Head

For the building up of the organic Body of Christ, firstly there is the need of Christ as the Head. In order to have a body, you must first have a head; this head is Christ Himself. Christ being the Head is through His overcoming, which is His death and resurrection. He defeated the enemy on the cross and through death destroyed the Devil who has the power of death. Moreover, He came out of Hades by overcoming death, and then He ascended to the heavens. Through the victory of His death and resurrection, as well as His ascension and exaltation, He captured the captives and perfected the gifted ones. Originally, we were those chosen by God before the foundation of the world; however, due to the fall, Satan had captured us through sin and put us into death. But God has not forsaken us; He Himself became flesh, passed through death, resurrection, and ascension to deal with our sins, to destroy Satan, to abolish death, and to capture us from the hands of Satan that we may sit together with Him in the heavens. It was in this kind of setting that we were redeemed, regenerated, and received the life of God and the Holy Spirit. Here we are being transformed and are growing; thus, some become the gifted persons. Peter, Paul, and the many apostles, prophets, evangelists, and shepherds and teachers, were all this kind of persons.

Following this, Christ gave these gifted ones to His Body. This was so not only during the apostles' age, but also throughout the generations. Among the thousands of believers, the Lord has perfected many gifted persons: some became apostles, some became prophets, some became evangelists, and some became shepherds and teachers. These the Lord gives to the church for the building up of the Body of Christ.

Needing the Gifted Ones

These gifted ones, the apostles, prophets, evangelists, shepherds and teachers, are perfected by the Head, Christ; these are needed by the Body. Their work is not to build up the church directly, but to perfect the saints so that they can also do the work of ministry, to build up the Body of Christ. Although the direction of the work of these four groups of people is different, their goal is the same, that is, the building up of the Body of Christ, yet not directly, but through the perfecting of the saints. The old way in the tradition of Christianity is to have a pastor do the preaching and a sanctified class of people do the holy work; the church is built by a clerical class, while the thousands of congregational members are not the builders. However, the new way ordained by God is carried out by a few gifted members who do not build up the church directly, but perfect every saint to do their work, which is the work of ministry, the building up of the Body of Christ.

What we have to do in the new way is to perfect the saints. The former old way only required the brothers and sisters to come to the meetings and listen to messages. As a result, decades have passed and not many have been perfected. It is as if we were conducting spiritual education for the last few decades, yet today not many have graduated, and not many teachers have been produced, so that it is difficult for us to increase and spread. This adequately proves that our way had problems. Therefore, we have to change to take the new way to perfect the saints.

Although the work of all the gifted ones may differ, they are all for the perfecting of the saints. For example, to be an apostle implies primarily three things: (1) pioneering to preach the gospel and bring people to the Lord; (2) establishing churches; (3) setting doctrinal principles and expounding the truths. The apostles are those who not only can do these things, but who also perfect others to do what they do. The prophets are also like this. They not only speak for God, and speak forth God, but also perfect others to be prophets. We also have the need of the evangelists among us today to lead the brothers and sisters in how to preach the gospel by knocking on doors, and to seek out the sons of peace among the wolves. All this requires practice, so even the more, they need to do the work of perfecting. There are also shepherds and teachers who are those taking care of people, shepherding people, and teaching people. Similarly, they need to go to perfect others to cause more and more saints to be able to do these things.

Therefore, brothers and sisters, the new way is a way which allows the gifted ones in the church to perfect all the saints. First, they perfect each one of the saints to be able to preach the gospel and to bring people to the Lord. Following that, they set up meetings in the new believers' homes and lead them to testify for the Lord, to read the Lord's Word, and even to speak for the Lord. Then they learn to care for one another, to feed one another, and to function organically. If we would learn humbly and practice faithfully according to this way revealed in the Bible, with all of the gifted ones—the apostles, prophets, evangelists, and shepherds and teachers—going to lead every believer to do these four things and to perfect them to do these things, then among the saints there will be an abundance of those who are apostles, prophets, evangelists, and shepherds and teachers. What a blessing the church will receive.

Needing the Perfected Members

For the sake of building up the organic body of Christ, all the perfected saints need to hold the truth in love, that is, to hold to the real things such as God, Christ, the Spirit, life, and the church, so that we can grow up into the Head, Christ. Then, out of the Head we will have something real which is for the building up of His Body. Then through every joint of the rich supply and through the operation of the measure of each one part, the whole Body can be joined and knit together to cause the growth and increase of the Body of Christ so that she builds herself up in love. When every member is thus perfected, growing in life, functioning organically, and being built up into a Body in the organic union, the Lord will have an organic Body in our midst to be His full expression. What a glorious and blessed situation that will be. I hope that all the brothers and sisters can see this vision clearly and pray for this that they themselves may become blessed persons on this God-ordained way, manifest the organic functions, and be built up in the organic Body of Christ.

When you have this desire, you will need to get into many things and learn in each matter. Learn how to preach the gospel, learn how to speak for the Lord, learn how to care for people, and also learn how to perfect others to do these things. You also need to learn to be apostles pioneering to establish churches and expounding the truths. Thus, every saved person among us, and whoever walks in this God-ordained way, will be functioning and will know how to preach the gospel, speak for the Lord, shepherd, and perfect others. As a result of this, the church will greatly expand, and the Lord will have a built up and organic Body. May we all see the goal of this new way accurately, endeavor wholeheartedly, learn seriously, overthrow the old way, and walk in this God-ordained way.

(Spoken by Witness Lee on April 20, 1988 in Taipei, Taiwan)

CHAPTER TWO

THE PRACTICAL STEPS OF GOD'S ORDAINED WAY

Scripture Reading: Luke 10:1-3, 5-7; 19:5; Acts 2:46; 5:42; 1 Cor. 14:26, 31, 1, 4b

OUTLINE

I. Preaching the gospel to gain people:
   A. By visiting people—Luke 10:1-3, 5-7:
      1. Needing to pay a price.
      2. Being sent as lambs into the midst of wolves.
      3. Finding the sons of peace.
   B. Bringing salvation to people's homes—Luke 19:5, 9.
II. Perfecting new believers:
   A. Setting up meetings in new believers' homes.
   B. Continuing steadfastly to meet with new believers.
   C. Leading new believers to function in meetings.
III. Establishing group meetings:
   A. Gradually bringing the new believers to form a group meeting.
   B. Leading new believers to fellowship and care for one another mutually.
   C. Leading them further to speak for the Lord in the meeting.
IV. Arriving at the practice of the district meetings:
   A. Gradually bringing the cared-for ones into district meetings.
   B. Helping the cared-for ones to get further into the church life.
   C. Leading the cared-for ones to speak for the Lord and to speak forth the Lord in district meetings.
   D. Through the saints' organic functioning, mutual speaking and supplying, and mutual establishing to build up the Body of Christ.

We have already seen that the goal of the new way is to build up the Body of Christ. Building up the Body of Christ is an organic function, not an organizational work. Like our human body, it is not by outward organizational means that the Body is sustained, but by the inward organic function of each part. The church is the Body of Christ; it is altogether organic. Every brother and sister is a member of this Body, that is, an organic part with an organic function within. This Bible-revealed, God-ordained new way that the Lord has shown us is to build up the organic Body of Christ through the organic functions.

PREACHING THE GOSPEL TO GAIN PEOPLE

The first major step in God's ordained way is preaching the gospel to gain people. In visiting people to preach the gospel to gain them for the Lord, we not only desire that people be saved, but also that they become the material for the building up of the Body of Christ. They must repent and be regenerated; then they must be transformed and grow up. Regeneration, transformation, and growing up are all organic matters. These are included in the organic building up.

For many years in the past, the way we preached the gospel was for the church to set the date for a gospel campaign. We passed out tracts and pasted up posters. Then the brothers and sisters were burdened to endeavor to invite relatives, friends, neighbors, schoolmates, and colleagues. Though we exerted great effort, it was often without much good result. You cannot say that this way is not a right way or a useful way, since there is such a gathering of people for the gospel from the Bible. However, if you study the Bible carefully, you will see the basic thought in gospel preaching is to go to where the sinners are. The Lord wants us to be the fishers of men (Matt. 4:19), indicating that the gospel preachers are fishermen. Which fishermen, instead of going to the ponds or sea to fish, send invitations asking fish to come to them? The Bible shows us that the Lord Jesus Himself came from the heavens to visit us. He visited people village by village and even house to house. Afterwards, He sent twelve disciples to visit people (Matt. 10:5), and later He sent out seventy (Luke 10:1). For lambs to visit wolves is not an easy thing—not only is there no blessing, but they must be prepared to encounter hardships and even scoldings.

We who have gone out to preach the gospel by visiting have all had such experiences. Sometimes we meet people who really are like "wolves"; but other times, when the door is opened, the people inside welcome us joyfully, and we know at first glance that they are sons of peace. By just a little speaking, they immediately believe and are baptized and thus are saved. There are many wonderful stories about meeting the sons of peace while preaching the gospel by visiting. (We hope to publish a periodical to relate these testimonies.) There are over one thousand churches around the world, and most are practicing this way of preaching the gospel by visiting. There have already been over a hundred thousand people who have believed and been baptized since the second half of 1986 through the preaching of the gospel by visiting. Even some other Christian groups have been influenced by us and are practicing preaching the gospel by visiting.

We used to invite twenty to thirty guests to hear the gospel and not even two would show up. Now we go to knock at twenty to thirty doors, and at least one person will be brought to salvation. This is the scientific way of working, and it is very effective. However, it is not easy to carry this out. It requires us to pay a price to lay down our status. We must believe that the Holy Spirit is with us, and we must speak the Lord's word to people, sentence by sentence, by the spirit. Some people are very rough with us at the start, but after our preaching they not only repent, pray, and believe, but also are baptized. Truly in an instant, wolves become lambs. We have spent one and a half years with hundreds of people, concentrating on experimenting with this matter. As a result, we have the proof that this is the most workable and effective way.

The secret in preaching the gospel by visiting is to be thick-skinned and tenacious. No matter how people revile you, your countenance is not changed, and no matter how much your head is hit, it is not broken. First you need to pray, confess thoroughly, ask for the cleansing of the Lord's blood to get the filling of the Holy Spirit, and offer yourself to the Holy Spirit that He will go out with you. Then, you will surely have the boldness and be full of authority. You can declare to the heaven and earth that you are going out with the Lord Christ to preach the gospel to sinners, commanding them to believe that they may be saved. You can even command demons to leave the homes which you are about to visit. Because the Lord said all authority in heaven and on earth has been given to Him, therefore, we should go and disciple the nations with this authority, baptizing them into the name of the Father, the Son, and the Holy Spirit. This is not a small thing.

All in all, we have rightly seen that this is the correct way. If we want to preach the gospel to people, we must go to the people. Who will go if you and I do not go? Who can God send? God cannot send the angels, since in the New Testament God did not become an angel but a man. God became flesh to move together with us. If we would not move, God has no way. Hence, we need to go to bring salvation to people's homes, just as the Lord Jesus brought salvation to Zaccheus' home.

PERFECTING THE NEW BELIEVERS

The second big step is to perfect the new believers. In our preaching the gospel by visiting, we bring people to believe in the Lord and we baptize them; then they become new believers. Now they are new born babes, and what they need most is care, which is also the perfecting. In the past we have been short in this matter, because most brothers and sisters have not been under such leading and perfecting to enable them to lead and perfect new believers. Although we have sometimes cared for them, visited them, and encouraged them to come to meetings in the meeting hall, the result has not been encouraging. This is because we did not see clearly that what God wanted was not to compel people to come to the meetings, but rather to bring the meetings to their homes. When we visit people, it is to bring the gospel of salvation to people. In the same way, when we perfect them after they are saved, it is to bring the meetings to their homes. We cannot expect that bringing the meetings to them two or three times will be sufficient, just as we cannot feed a newborn babe only two or three times. We were not clear about this in the past. So, although we have baptized many, only a few are left. This time we have learned the lesson. As we go back to the Bible, we see that immediately after people are saved and baptized, we need to meet with them in their homes.

Therefore, we should not leave a new one right away after we baptize him. We need to spend at least half an hour to an hour to lead a newly baptized one to know that today Christ as the Savior is the Spirit, even the life-giving Spirit, and that He entered into his spirit at the moment he believed, to enliven his spirit and to cause him to be regenerated. Simply speak to him in this way according the Bible, show him the related verses, and then lead him to pray and use his spirit to call on the name of the Lord to contact the Lord Spirit. Afterwards, go back every two or three days for a month. Use ten home meetings to work into him the basic Christian knowledge and experience in order to lay a good foundation of life. Then change the home meeting frequency to once a week, or at least once every other week, caring for him this way for as long as a year. In the process you must tell him that we are not professional preachers, but only those who have had the Lord's grace and are constrained by the Lord's love to bring people to be saved, to grow, and to be perfected by the Lord. We are the same as they are, all being brothers in the church, meeting and functioning together. For this reason, bring them to learn all that we do in the meetings. Bit by bit they can learn to pray, to call hymns, to speak the hymns, to read the Bible, and to speak for the Lord, thereby developing their organic ability.

ESTABLISHING GROUP MEETINGS

The third major step is to establish group meetings. First we have meetings in the new believers' homes. Perhaps after one or two months, they would like to meet other Christians. We could then bring three to five nearby new believers together and establish a group meeting. As the saints know one another, they will encourage and establish one another. Meanwhile there will be the bond of love, the mutual fellowship, and the mutual care. Moreover, there will be the opportunity for all to manifest the organic ability in each one by speaking for the Lord and testifying for the Lord.

It is hard for a single piece of coal to start burning, but by putting a pile of coals together, they will burn, and the more they burn, the hotter and the bigger the fire will get. Needless to say, men are social beings. They do not like to be alone. The best gathering is a Christian gathering, where you are not only undefiled and away from evil deeds, but you also enjoy grace and know the truth. What was originally meetings in homes becomes a group meeting, where people can be more interested in reading the Bible and be more encouraged to love the Lord. They can learn from the Bible reading and can experience the Lord in loving Him. Spontaneously they have more to testify of and can further speak for the Lord in the meetings.

ARRIVING AT THE PRACTICE OF THE DISTRICT MEETINGS

The fourth step is arriving at the practice of the district meetings. We still need to gradually bring the new believers from the group meetings to the district meetings to help them come further into the church life. The meeting content is richer in the district meetings. There is the breaking of the bread to remember the Lord, the learning of the truths, as well as the mutual fellowship and sharing. Everyone has more opportunity to function, to speak for the Lord, and to edify one another. We all can also have a higher enjoyment, hear more complete messages, and obtain a more perfect edification and comprehensive building up. Therefore, we ought to inspire the ones we are helping, to speak for the Lord and to speak forth the Lord in the district meetings. Then all the saints in the meeting can function organically, speak to supply one another, and edify mutually, and thus build up the Body of Christ.

I have given you a sketch hoping we all may see that the practical steps in building up the Body of Christ are completely different from the organized ways of religion. The way of organized religion is to get together, collect some capital, and hire a preacher or pastor to bear a particular responsibility and do a particular work. Most there merely offer some financial support and have no direct relation with this work. Among us, however, it is not so. As soon as we bring people to salvation, we should meet in their homes, lead them to call on the name of the Lord, lead them to pray-read the Word, and bring them closer to the Lord. As they grow in life, spontaneously they will speak and testify for the Lord. They do this not for money or gain, but spontaneously they have an organic function because they have the Lord's life and the Lord's Spirit within them. If, in a local church, quite a few brothers and sisters all function organically by the ability of the inward life, the effect will surely be living and organic.

Through participating in the home meetings, the group meetings, and the district meetings, it will take about a year for a new believer to go from being saved and baptized to functioning a little in the district meeting. At this time we can hand him over to the care of the church to be built up in the Body of Christ. He then will become a useful member and will lead others in the same way. He will also be able to care for, lead, perfect, and meet others' needs. This way of "teachers bringing up students" will raise up many useful persons. The new way that the Lord is leading us into is indeed an organic way. Those raised up in this way are naturally organic. Contained in our preaching of the gospel by visiting people to give freely the grace which we have obtained freely is the life power with the organic ability. Further on in this way, an organic entity, which is the church in a locality, will develop. This church is the local expression of the universal Body of Christ, and her functioning in the locality is not organizational but organic.

EVERYONE PRACTICING THE NEW WAY

We all love the Lord and are concerned for the Lord's move. We know that the Lord's building up of His Body is not accomplished just by a few gifted persons. It takes all those who belong to the Lord, who are motivated by the Lord's love, to bear their share in preaching the gospel by visiting, perfecting the new believers, establishing the group meetings, and arriving at the practice of the district meetings. Only thus can the Body of Christ be built up.

Today, the practical steps of the new way have already been put before us. This is now our responsibility. As long as there are one thousand saints in Taipei who would receive this word, pay the price, exert themselves, put themselves willingly in the Lord's move, and practice the new way according to the Lord's leading, the situation in the church will be greatly improved. The church will have a dynamic spreading, and the Body of Christ will also be properly built up.

As an illustration, in a place with one hundred meeting together, we hope there would be thirty who are motivated by the Lord's love to be willing to take the Lord's leading to practice the new way step by step. Grouped in threes, with different ages and sexes, they would coordinate to preach the gospel by visiting people. Doing so every other week, for two hours each time, they can bring one to salvation in a month. They can bring twelve people to be saved in a year, since there are twelve months in a year. Thus, thirty saints, divided into ten teams, can in one year bring a hundred and twenty people to be saved, which is more than the original number. Then they can lead the new believers to have home, group, and district meetings. Even if we figure that two out of four will be lost, eventually there will be sixty remaining out of the one hundred and twenty. Thus the rate of increase is still sixty percent. In addition, this place of one hundred saints can support at least two or three full-timers. They, laboring this way, can also bring in fifty. Adding the two together, there will be one hundred and ten added in a year. This is quite a considerable number.

Concerning the weekly meeting schedule, we can arrange it in the following way. The district meeting will be on the Lord's Day morning to break the bread for remembering the Lord, to learn the truths, and to fellowship and share. The prayer and service meeting will be on Tuesday to cry out to the Lord for the new way with one accord. Then, either preach the gospel by visiting people or go to a home or a group meeting on two other evenings to bear the responsibility for caring for and perfecting the saints. If we all do this willingly, faithfully, and with much labor, the church in Taipei will be on the track of the organic way. The whole church life will be organic and not organizational, and it will belong to all the saints, not to just a few. In this way, it will be a prosperous and blessed situation, and the effect will be glorious and bountiful.

(A message given by Brother Witness Lee on April 21, 1988 in Taipei)

Chapter Three

THE DIVINE POWER OF GOD AND THE PRECIOUS PROMISES OF THE LORD

Scripture Reading: 2 Pet. 1:3-11; 2 Cor. 12:9; Matt. 6:31-33; Phil. 4:19

OUTLINE

I. The divine power of God—2 Pet. 1:3:
   A. Through our knowing the One who has called us through His own glory and virtue.
   B. Having given to us all things which relate to life and godliness:
      1. Life being the inward divine supply—with God as life.
      2. Godliness being the outward divine expression —God lived out.
II. The precious promises of the Lord—2 Pet. 1:4:
   A. Through His glory and virtue.
   B. The Lord having granted to us precious and exceedingly great promises.
   C. That we having escaped the corruption which is in the world by lust.
   D. That through these promises we might become partakers of the divine nature.
III. Our diligent cooperation—2 Pet. 1:5-11:
   A. Upon the seed of the like precious faith allotted to us, through six steps, developing to the love which is God—2 Pet. 1:1, 5-7.
   B. Constituting us neither idle nor unfruitful—2 Pet. 1:8.
   C. Making our calling and selection firm—2 Pet. 1:10.
   D. Being richly and bountifully supplied to enter into the eternal kingdom of the Lord—2 Pet. 1:11.

This is a training message for the working brothers and sisters. When I was seeking before the Lord on your behalf, I felt that if the working brothers and sisters are to be adequately and properly participating in the church life, they need to receive the life supply continuously. What you need is not so much to do something, to learn something, or to bear some burdens. What you need is mainly to receive the life supply. If there is not the adequate supply to our physical life, it will be difficult for us to walk, not to mention to bear burdens. It is the same with our spiritual life. The most important thing is to obtain the life supply.

GOD HAVING THE REQUIREMENTS, YET EVEN THE MORE, THE SUPPLY

In the Bible, there are many places that speak about God's requirements. For example, there were the requirements of the laws in the Old Testament. However, due to the inability of man to keep the laws by himself, there is Christ as grace to supply us in the New Testament. Furthermore, the first book of the Gospels, the Gospel of Matthew, is not a book of supply, but a book of requirements. Moreover, its requirements are higher than the requirements of the law; they are the kingdom requirements. Matthew 5, 6, and 7 show us that these kingdom requirements surpass the requirements of the law. The requirements of the law are of the letter, but the kingdom requirements are of life. Unless a person has the life of God, he will definitely not be able to keep them. This would be like asking a dog to live like a person; this is not feasible. If a dog is to work like a man and live like a man, then it must have the life of a man. Not only does it need to have the life of a man, but also the life supply of a man. Hence, following Matthew, when you get to John, there are no more requirements, but rather the supply. This shows us that the law requires, but grace supplies; the kingdom requires, but life supplies. The Lord came to be this life supply so that we can meet the requirements of the kingdom, live the kingdom life, be the kingdom people, and fulfill God's eternal purpose on the earth.

The Bible fully presents to us these two matters of

requirement and supply. There is no doubt that God requires of us, but God does not expect us to fulfill this requirement by ourselves. First, He requires of us in order to show us that we are not able. Then He comes into us to be our life in order to supply us so that we can meet His requirements and fulfill His eternal purpose. This is an ironclad principle in the Bible. Outwardly speaking, the church life is a requirement to us. It requires us to pay a price, but in reality we are enjoying, and we obtain Christ as our supply.

Besides the four Gospels and the book of Acts, the other twenty-two books in the New Testament tell us about the supply we enjoy in the church life so that we can satisfy God's requirements. What we enjoy is Christ Himself, and this Christ is the embodiment of the Triune God. All the riches and the fullness of the Triune God dwell in Christ. Today this Christ is the life-giving Spirit within us to be our life for supplying us. Only by this life supply can we carry out our commission before God in order to satisfy God's requirements.

There is a portion of the Word in 2 Peter 1 which is most fitting to the need of those who enjoy the Lord in the church life today. It says that the divine power of God has already granted to us all things related to life and godliness. Moreover, in order for us to enjoy this life and live out this godliness, He has also given to us the precious and exceedingly great promises. He did not only grant us life and godliness within, but He also granted us a New Testament without. In this testament there is God and there are the precious and exceedingly great promises. These promises tell us that although the requirements of our God are so high, He wants to completely fulfill them within us and upon us. Therefore, we do not have to bear a heavy burden or be worrisome for living the church life. All we need to do is enjoy the Lord in a simple way. Then, however the Lord leads within us, we will just do it. There is just enjoyment and work with no laboring, heavy burdens, or worries. God's supply always follows God's requirement. If God has a requirement, He will also have the supply. This is an ironclad principle and is the clear teaching of the Bible.

GOD HAVING GRANTED TO US ALL THINGS RELATED TO LIFE AND GODLINESS

All the ones sitting here are working saints. When I was young, I was also working. Because my background was poor, I had to work when I was a teenager. Afterwards, I got saved, and because of the Lord's calling and attracting, I was very happy being a Christian. Whether I was reading the Bible, praying, or preaching the gospel, I enjoyed it very much. But sometimes I read some words in the Bible which caused me to feel sad. For example, the Bible says, "You shall be holy, because I am holy" (1 Pet. 1:16). It also says, "You, therefore, shall be perfect as your heavenly Father is perfect" (Matt. 5:48). In another place it says, "Whoever does not carry his own cross and come after Me, cannot be My disciple" (Luke 14:27). I thought in my heart, "How can I be holy? How can I be perfect as my heavenly Father? To ask me to carry the cross to follow the Lord is an impossible task. However, I cannot just drop it and forget about it; it was not up to me to decide whether I should be a Christian." Therefore, I was really sad and full of worry.

My Christian life was like this year after year. More and more I found myself to be no good. If we still have some hope for ourselves, then it proves that we still consider ourselves to be all right. I finally reached a point where you may say that I knew myself thoroughly and realized that there was not even one bit of hope with me. I could not be holy, I could not follow the Lord, I could not overcome, I could not be spiritual, and I could not be perfect as God is perfect. I could not do it at all.

It was at this time that the light of the Bible enlightened me to see that God never said that we are all right. We are rotten to the core. It is impossible for us to be holy and perfect. When I was subdued, the life supply came. I saw that it was due to my being no good that I needed Jesus to be my life. Afterwards when I went to read the Bible, the situation was different. What had formerly been words of requirement in the Bible was all changed in my reading to become words of supply. I remember that one time about thirty years ago when I was working in Manila, as I was reading 2 Peter 1, I was greatly opened up to see that the divine power of God has already granted to us all things related to life and godliness. Life and godliness include sanctification, perfection, spirituality, overcoming, and all the requirements in the Bible. Therefore, we do not have to worry, because all these have already been granted to us.

DRAWING ON GOD'S SUPPLY BY FAITH

I know that many working brothers and sisters, after finding a job, experience pressure from their boss, competition from their co-workers, plus the jealousy of the aggressive ones. It is indeed not a simple situation. Not only so, but after marriage they will have a wife, and not long afterwards they will have children. It is indeed troublesome. Although there is enjoyment in these things, yet it is not without troubles. What shall we do? This is just like the hymn we sang tonight, which says,

> Thou art all my life, Lord,
> In me Thou dost live;
> With Thee all God's fulness
> Thou to me dost give.
> By Thy holy nature
> I am sanctified,
> By Thy resurrection,
> Vict'ry is supplied.

The last stanza says,

> I would cease completely
> From my efforts vain,
> Let Thy life transform me,
> Full release to gain.
>   (*Hymns*, #841)

This is just like what the Bible shows us. The divine power of God has granted unto us all things related to life and godliness. The sufficient life supply will meet all our needs. Therefore, we do not have to worry; we need only to draw on God's supply by faith.

Second Peter 1 opens by saying that we have been allotted like precious faith from God. Through this faith, all the things related to life and godliness will become reality to us, and we will be led into this reality. The divine nature will also become the element of our Christian living and experience. Then holiness and perfection are not hard matters to us; even overcoming and being spiritual are very easy. This is like my sitting inside a 747 jumbo jet flying from Taipei to Los Angeles. I will get there after flying for fourteen hours. Actually, it was not I who was flying; I was merely enjoying. Similarly, what delivered Noah and his eight family members from the destruction by the flood was not Noah himself, but the ark. The ark delivered them from the judgment of the flood; yet they themselves were inside enjoying God's preparation.

Today our Christian life is also like this. Everything in Christ is an enjoyment. If we are not in Christ, our being a working one is a heavy burden. Marriage and rearing up children are all burdens. What a suffering it is! Therefore, we should not forget that the beginning of 2 Peter 1 tells us that the divine power of God has already granted to us all things related to life and godliness. God within us is our life, and He is also supplying us day by day.

The sad thing is that although we have Christ as the "747," we often do not get onto the plane. We have Christ as the ark, yet we often do not go in. We still try to use our own efforts and schemes, yet the result is that we bring to ourselves burdens and difficulties. Then how do we get onto the spiritual "747"? How do we enter into the ark? As long as we are contacting Christ, it does not matter where we are or what time it is, because He belongs to us. First Corinthians 10:4 says that the Israelites in the Old Testament had a living rock following them, which was Christ. Today Christ as the real rock is following us. We may contact Him at any time. We may call on Him from our heart at any time, "O Lord Jesus!" Even though one call seems so simple, yet it is really something; we can get the deliverance. Just by our calling, we enjoy the Lord as life within, and we will manifest godliness without. When we call on Him unceasingly in this way, although we do not see Him outwardly, yet in our spirit we can contact Him and enjoy our organic union with Him. By this He becomes our content and supply.

We have to realize that all of our problems occur because our union with the Lord is broken. If the electricity stops in the day to day life, the lights, sound, and air conditioning will all be gone. We will not be able to do anything. But as long as the electricity is connected, all of these will be available. This is a very good illustration. Sometimes we may be wrong and may not be clear concerning the Lord's leading. This is the result of our fellowship with the Lord being broken and of our having lost the joy and the peace within. I have had many human experiences and also a lot of difficulties. For example, I have many children and many grandchildren. All these are burdens. So I have only one way, which is to contact the Lord and call on Him. As soon as I call, immediately I get the enjoyment and feel happy and peaceful.

THE LORD GRANTING TO US THE PRECIOUS AND EXCEEDINGLY GREAT PROMISES

The divine power of our God has already granted to us all things related to life and godliness (2 Pet. 1:3). This granting is something living. It is like an electric current flowing into us. It was by this divine power that God called us. We were drawn like being caught by a fishing line. This is what it means by the Lord's calling us through His glory and virtue. From now on, we are like a fish hooked and caught; we cannot run away any longer. This is the calling of God. It was the glory and virtue of God that captured us. Moreover, through this glory and virtue, He granted unto us precious and exceedingly great promises (1:4). This word *virtue* in the original language means excellency, denoting the energy of life to overcome all obstacles and to carry out all excellent attributes. When we heard the gospel, were enlightened, and called on the Lord Jesus, there was something attracting us within, causing us to feel that the Lord is good, glorious, and excellent. This is the Lord's virtue becoming our calling through which He granted to us many promises.

We may say that every word of the entire New Testament is a promise. I have selected two of the more obvious portions.

First, on the spiritual side, Paul said in 2 Corinthians 12 that he had a thorn in his flesh causing him to suffer. He prayed three times to the Lord that the thorn might depart from him. But the Lord said to him, "My grace is sufficient for you, for My power is perfected in weakness" (vv. 7-9). This shows us that the Lord's grace and power were sufficient to sustain and supply Paul and bring him through these sufferings and difficulties. Therefore, Paul said that he would rather boast in his weaknesses so that the power of Christ might tabernacle over him. The original meaning of the word *tabernacle* here is to fix a tent or a habitation upon something. This portrays the power of Christ, which is Christ Himself, being like a tent tabernacling over us, overshadowing our weaknesses.

Every time when we feel heavily burdened, we need to listen to the Lord's voice saying, "My grace is sufficient for you. My power is perfected in weakness." If we consider ourselves to be strong, then we will not be able to enjoy the Lord's power. Therefore, our weakness is precious. It is due to our weaknesses that the Lord's power has the ground to manifest itself and we are able to enjoy His power. What a promise this is!

Concerning material things, the Lord said in Matthew 6, "Therefore do not be anxious, saying, What shall we eat? or, What shall we drink? or, With what shall we be clothed? For all these things the nations are seeking; for your heavenly Father knows that you need all these things. But seek first His kingdom and His righteousness, and all these things shall be added to you" (vv. 31-33). Formerly I always prayed to the Lord concerning my daily needs. But gradually I became clear about the Lord's revelation. I do not need to pray for all these things; He knows all these things already, and He will take care of me as long as I seek first His kingdom and His righteousness. His kingdom is the church, and His righteousness is Christ.

As long as we seek first His kingdom and His righteousness, whatever we might need, He will add to us. He will not only give us the kingdom and the righteousness, but also will add to us whatever we need in our living, such as what we need to eat, drink, and clothe ourselves with. I have not yet seen a person who followed the Lord die of hunger or freezing. I have only seen those who love the Lord and experience the Lord being richly clothed and adequately fed. Therefore, we do not need to worry about our living, because this is altogether in His hand. We should do our duty and work diligently, experiencing the Lord as the overshadowing power within us. At the same time, we should also believe that He will bear the responsibility regarding all our outward circumstances, daily needs, and financial arrangements.

Therefore, in the way we use our time, we should also have some arrangement. You work five and a half days a week. Each day, besides working, eating, and resting, there are at least two hours which can be used, plus half a day on Saturday and a whole day on the Lord's Day. These times can be used for serving the Lord, for preaching the gospel by visiting people, for caring for the saints, or for attending home meetings, group meetings, or district meetings. Even if there are some who, because of family burdens, need to work two jobs, I absolutely believe that regardless of how busy they are during the week, they can set apart at least half a day to attend a meeting. This is altogether dependent on our feeling and our viewpoint toward things.

God's creation follows a set of laws. If a person knows only to work, without adequate rest, then it will not be too long before he cannot make it anymore. Man also needs to have entertainment. According to my human experience, the best and the highest entertainment is to live the church life. The church life not only gives people joy and satisfaction, but also uplifts the standard of morality of human beings. Although many worldly entertainments do afford pleasure, yet they may cause us to suffer loss, or even to be defiled by downgrading our morality. Only the church life causes us to be blessed. It is beneficial to our body, heart, and spirit. If in our whole life we do not practice the church life, love the Lord, and serve the Lord, then not only is there a great effect on ourselves, our family, and our children, but the loss we will suffer is beyond estimation.

PARTAKING OF GOD'S NATURE THROUGH GOD'S PROMISE

God has already granted to us precious and exceedingly great promises that we may escape the corruption that is in the world by lust. Then through these promises, we can partake of God's nature and enjoy God's essence which is love. As long as we receive these promises of God, He can cause us to escape the corruption that is in the world by lust and to practice the church life in peace, enjoying Christ and being happy and joyful.

Dear brothers and sisters, I would speak a word of love to you. You should take the attitude that as long as there are clothes to wear and there is food to eat, you should be content and carry out your duty to practice the church life and enjoy Christ according to what you have learned and experienced. All the other things are in His hand; we do not need to plan for them. Because the worldly people do not have the Lord and His promises, they have to plan and worry for everything. But we have a Father in heaven who thinks about us and bears our responsibility. All we need is to live in His promises and do our duty, restfully and stably enjoying His presence and His divine essence. What a blessing this is!

DILIGENTLY COOPERATING WITH GOD

Second Peter 1 continues by saying that we need to cooperate with God and work with God diligently. He has already allotted to us like precious faith. We have to go forward to develop this faith, to supply in our faith virtue, and in virtue knowledge, and in knowledge self-control, and in self-control endurance, and in endurance godliness, and in godliness brotherly love, and in brotherly love the love of God.

When we have such an enjoyment of God, these things will exist within us and abound. They will constitute us neither idle nor unfruitful. The Lord in John 15 says, "I am the vine, you are the branches" (v. 5). The branches are for fruit bearing. Therefore, we need only to exercise the allotted faith so that the virtues of the divine life can be developed step by step to reach maturity unto the bearing of fruit to glorify God. This will cause our calling and election to be steadfast.

Eventually, we will obtain the rich and bountiful supply to enter into the eternal kingdom of our Lord and Savior Jesus Christ for the reward of the kingdom, the enjoyment of His kingship, and the joy with Him in the kingdom. These are the precious promises we received from the Lord and also the living we ought to have by the divine power of God.

(Spoken by Brother Witness Lee on April 16, 1988 in Taipei)

CHAPTER FOUR

THE MIRACULOUSLY NORMAL LIVING IN THE NEW WAY

Scripture Reading: Heb. 7:25; Phil. 1:19; 4:13; Heb. 3:12

OUTLINE

I. Being revived every morning:
   A. Calling on the Lord and contacting the Lord immediately upon rising up in the morning.
   B. Enjoying the Lord and absorbing the Lord's rich supply using a few verses.
II. Living an overcoming life daily:
   A. Calling on the Lord unceasingly—Rom. 10:12.
   B. Dealing with sins and being filled with the Spirit at all times.
   C. Walking according to spirit—Rom. 8:4.
   D. Living Christ—Phil. 1:21.
   E. Speaking the Lord in any place at any time—2 Tim. 4:2.
III. Gaining people by preaching the gospel:
   A. Going to visit people twice a month.
   B. Going out two hours each time.
IV. Perfecting the new believers:
   A. Setting up a meeting in new believers' homes—Acts 2:46; 5:42.
   B. Leading the new believers to go on in the spiritual life and to function in the meetings.
V. Leading a small number of believers:
   A. Setting up group meetings.
   B. Leading the new believers to have contact and fellowship with neighboring saints in the group meetings.

    C. Leading the new believers to go on further in functioning in the group meetings by speaking for the Lord.
VI. Participating in the district meetings:
    A. Striving to speak for the Lord and speak forth the Lord—1 Cor. 14:26, 31.
    B. Exercising to be in the same flow and to coordinate with the saints in speaking for the Lord.
    C. Supplying to perfect the saints, building up the Body of Christ—Eph. 4:12.

GOD BREATHING OUT AND WE BREATHING IN

In the New Testament, there is the thought that we can breathe God in. For example, in 2 Timothy 3:16 where the Apostle Paul was talking about the origin of the Bible, he said that the Bible is God-breathed. This indicates that when we are reading God's Word, God is breathing out toward us; He breathes out and we breathe in. Not only so, but in both the Old Testament and the New Testament, the word for "spirit" in Hebrew and Greek has a threefold meaning: spirit, wind, and breath. The Lord said in John 3:6, "That which is born of the Spirit is spirit." Verse 8 also says, "The wind blows where it wills, and you hear the sound of it, but you do not know where it comes from and where it is going; so is everyone who is born of the Spirit." The wind in this verse and the Spirit in verse 6 are the same word in Greek.

Genesis 2:7 shows us that when God created Adam, He used the dust of the ground to form the shape of a body and then breathed the breath of life into his nostrils, and he became a living person with a spirit. When we come to John 20, after the Lord died and resurrected, He appeared to the disciples and breathed into them saying, "Receive the Holy Spirit" (v. 22). From this we can see that the Bible, from the Old Testament to the New, has the thought that God is breath to us.

However, this is not the religious thought concerning God. The religionists consider God as someone great and unlimited; they only take God as an object of worship, as someone supreme and grand. We human beings are low and have no way to contact God; God is someone far away from us. But the revelation of the Bible shows us that God to us is a matter of breath; this matter is also of the Spirit. Romans 10:8 says that this resurrected Christ has become the living Word, being near to us, even in our mouth and in our heart. Just consider a little. If our great God is not breath, how can He be in our mouth, and how can He enter into our heart? Today many people have a wrong view of God and misunderstand God, thinking that God is so great that He is unapproachable. In John 4 the Lord Jesus was talking with a Samaritan woman about the matter of worshipping God. The woman said, "Our fathers worshipped in this mountain, and you say that in Jerusalem is the place where men should worship." Jesus told her that God is Spirit and those who worship Him must worship neither in this mountain nor in Jerusalem, but in spirit and in reality (vv. 20-24). Therefore, for us to worship God is to contact God the Spirit in our human spirit.

You may say that we have already heard a lot of this kind of teaching in the Lord's recovery, but unconsciously these things seem to have vanished in our living. This is because we have been too deeply influenced by the traditional religious thinking that God is too great, too solemn, and too majestic. Although there is nothing wrong with this aspect, God is also practical; He is breath. He breathes out, and we breathe in; this breathing in and breathing out is life. Hymn #255 speaks specifically about this. Because the writer of the hymn had such an appreciation and experience of the Lord, he said in the chorus, "I am breathing out my sorrow, breathing out my sin; I am breathing, breathing, breathing, all Thy fulness in." This kind of hymn is indeed profound; merely singing it will cause us to be cleansed and be washed from all the spots and wrinkles in our lives. Today if we can learn the secret—to come to the Lord to breathe Him in, to call on Him from deep within, to breathe in this breath of life of the Lord—then our spiritual life will surely be healthy.

A NORMAL LIVING YET MIRACULOUS

The title of this chapter, "The Miraculously Normal Living in the New Way," is based on the divine revelation of the Bible that we may have a living that breathes in God. Breathing is something too ordinary and too normal, not outstanding in any way, yet it is miraculous. We human beings can have God, not merely to be our outward help and support, but to enter into us to be our life and supply. This is truly an amazing fact. We all know that the most needful and most available thing to us is air. A person can live without eating or drinking for a few days, but he will be finished if he does not breathe for even a few minutes. Air is too precious, too needful. It costs nothing to buy and is available everywhere. This physical air signifies a spiritual thing; God is our real air. How simple it is for us to get air. In the same way, it is also simple for us to have God. Although it is simple to have God, yet it is miraculous that God enters into man to be his life and life supply.

I would like to point out one thing to you. The Christian life that we have is one that is normal, without one bit of peculiarity, yet it is also miraculous; it is a story of the Triune God living within us. In Philippians 4:12 the Apostle Paul testified, saying, "I know both how to be abased, and I know how to abound; in everything and in all things I have learned the secret both to be filled and to hunger, both to abound and to be in want." This word indicates that Paul had been poor, and he had been rich. When he was poor, he knew how to handle it; when he was rich, he also knew how to handle it. In my whole life, it has not been easy for me to see one person who really knows how to be in poverty and also how to be in abundance. Conversely, I saw many who could do well in poverty, yet when they became rich, they did not do so well. However, a Christian's normal living should be one that is fitting in every situation and every place; to a certain point, he is neither poor nor rich. In the process of his entire human living, Paul had learned the secret in everything. His secret is mentioned in the following verse, where he says, "I can do all things in Him who empowers me" (v. 13). The secret of our normal Christian life is a person, Christ Himself.

Today all the ones seated here are working brothers and sisters. I also have worked before; I know the difficulties of working. There are all kinds of pressures and all kinds of temptations. It is really not easy for the working ones to overcome. For this reason, I would like to fellowship two things with you. First, when Christians are suffering, having a difficult time, it is easier for them to depend on the Lord; however, when they are successful and are taking it easy, it becomes difficult for them. You need to know that during difficult times, there are not that many defeated Christians; during easy times, there are not many Christians who can stand, either. Second, the rarest and the most honorable Christians are those who can handle poverty as well as abundance. Not only so, they can handle the situation to a point that they are neither poor nor rich. For a Christian to maintain himself as neither poor nor rich is an exceptional matter.

Most of the working young people after graduating from school give their everything to struggle and endeavor to establish their families and their professions in order to prepare for their future. Everyone wants to be rich and live a life in abundance. Not only would they like to have comfortable houses, but also fancy automobiles. I am not here encouraging you to be rich; neither am I advising you to remain in the same position you are in now. I desire that you always practice to live a normal Christian life. This kind of life is neither poor nor rich, neither suffering nor comfortable. The Bible shows us that the living of the man created by God is one that has obligation, responsibility, duty, and enjoyment. His obligation, responsibility, and duty are for his existence, and his existence should be a kind of enjoyment. When a person is so poor, it is hard for him to have any enjoyment, but when a person becomes rich, neither does he necessarily have the real enjoyment. When you eat too well or dress too meticulously, you will nevertheless be troubled. There are some who if they have a lot of money, will spend it indiscriminately. This not only damages that person, but also others. It not only damages his own morality, but also the atmosphere of society. We Christians are not like this. We learn to live a life that is neither poor nor rich. We are content with being clothed and fed. We also enjoy the material living in a simple, quiet, comfortable, worry free, and trouble free manner. We are blessed ourselves, and it is beneficial to others.

THE LORD'S LIFE AND HIS PRECIOUS PROMISES

In the last chapter we saw that the divine power of God has granted to us all things related to life and godliness and has also granted to us precious and exceedingly great promises. Hence, we should not worry for the needs of our daily life. Rather, we need to calm down our desire and concern, so that we can escape the corruption that is in the world through lust and be partakers of the divine nature, to enjoy God Himself. The tide of this age, the pressure of living, the bondage of human affection, plus our own lust, both inwardly and outwardly are seducing us, constraining us, in order to ensnare us into corruption through lust. But we have the Lord's life and His promises. When we live by these, we can live peacefully and contentedly in the practical situation of our living. Our money and our time should also have proper arrangement and balance, affording help to man's need and God's business through proper means. Then we will have a living that really enjoys human life.

Only the life of Christ and His precious promises can cause us to live this kind of normal yet miraculous living. Through this we can save much money as well as time for prayer, fellowshipping with the Lord, enjoying the Lord in His Word, going out to preach the gospel to people by visiting them, and caring for the saints. I always bow my head to worship the Lord for what He has allotted to me. Due to His sovereign arrangement, He caused me to be born in a poor village and grow up in a poor home. From my youth, I learned to be hard working and enduring, endeavoring to move forward. Hence, I was also preserved. Afterwards in my studies, I came in contact with missionaries from whom I learned English and had more opportunity to know the Lord. After my graduation, the Lord caused my living to be not too poor nor too rich, but just right for serving the Lord. Because I knew English, I could know the Bible in a more convenient way, even making footnotes to the Bible, and expounding the truths. Nevertheless, I did not know English to the point that I could become an English professor or scholar. If I had pursued that, I would not have been able to concentrate on being the Lord's worker. For the Lord's sake, I have been in poverty, and I also have been in abundance. The Lord still caused me to be at peace. Speaking of earthly achievement, I do not possess anything today, and neither am I anything. I am just an ordinary person, preserved by the Lord and enjoying the genuine human life.

The Lord created and redeemed us, not for the purpose of making us someone special. What the Lord desires is that we live a proper and normal life, experiencing, enjoying, and expressing Him. The highest philosophy of human living is in the Bible. This kind of human life is normal yet miraculous because it is not something that we can live by ourselves, but God must enter into us to be our life in order for us to live out this kind of life. When the Lord Jesus was a man on the earth, He lived this kind of life. Before He came out to minister at the age of thirty, He was growing up in a despised city, in a carpenter's home. The Bible does not record what He did or said; He was just there living. That God who created everything, including mankind, would become an ordinary and humble human being in the flesh, without anything outstanding is a real miracle.

I can testify in this way: the Lord Jesus lives within me as my life. I am very satisfied in my living today. I feel that I am enjoying human life the most. I go to bed, rise up, eat, and drink on time. Hence, I have no woes or sicknesses. By the Lord's grace, I am already over eighty years old. I am still healthy. Not only can I take care of many business affairs, but I can also memorize the words of the Bible. I am speaking this word to you working ones so that you may know that our being able to live the church life on the earth is a most blessed matter. The church life is the most normal and miraculous living. Therefore, none of us saved ones may say that we do not have time to live the church life. If someone does not have time to live the church life, it is because he does not enjoy the Lord enough. As long as the Lord's supply within us is adequate, our church life will surely be proper and satisfying, and time will not become a problem.

Although we saved ones live in the world, we should not belong to the world. We were saved and delivered from the worldly falsehood and deceit. In this current of the world, not only do we not join others in their evil, but we also are able to stand and become a pillar in the midst of the current. I hope that these words can help you so that you can be strengthened in the Lord's grace. He has already granted to us all the supply. We should live in His living and stand on His promises, allowing His life and His promises to calm all the desires within us and remove all our demands. Then we can live our days in quietness and stability, living a normal church life, that we personally, our family, our relatives, and friends, and even the society may be blessed. This is what the Lord spoke in Matthew 5 when He said that we are the salt of the earth and the light of the world (vv. 13-14). We are salt because we can remove the corruption of the earth. We are light because we can enlighten the people in darkness. Nevertheless, any time we do not live the church life, we lose the taste and do not shine. Therefore, in order for us to maintain our status and function as salt and light, we must practice the church life in a good way.

THE LIVING IN THE NEW WAY

Following this, we come to see the outline of this chapter. Here, I will use very simple words to explain to you what the miraculously normal living in the new way is.

BEING REVIVED AND OVERCOMING

First, we must be revived every morning. At the end of a day is the night, and after the night is passed is the morning. Every morning we should have a revival from the Lord, a new beginning. For this reason, we should be calling on the Lord and contacting Him immediately upon rising in the morning, and enjoying the Lord and absorbing the His rich supply using two or three verses. Whether it is ten minutes or twenty minutes; it is still all right. It is like eating breakfast. At any rate, we have to eat the spiritual food every morning before the Lord so that our spirit is filled every day.

Second, we must live an overcoming life every day through calling on the Lord unceasingly (Rom. 10:12). Regardless how busy we are, we may still call from our heart, saying, "O Lord

Jesus!" We also must deal with sins and be filled with the Spirit at all times (Acts 13:52). As long as there is even a little in the way of trespasses, falsehood, or sins, we should confess and ask the Lord to cleanse us with His blood so that we can maintain the condition of being filled with the Spirit. Then, we walk according to spirit (Rom. 8:4). Our outward movement is governed by the inward spirit. We also live Christ (Phil. 1:21). This is our daily life. If we would practice the foregoing three items—calling on the Lord unceasingly, dealing with sins and being filled with the Spirit at all times, and walking according to spirit—spontaneously the issue is living Christ. Then we speak the Lord everywhere at every time (2 Tim. 4:2). Whether it is in season or out of season, whether it is convenient or inconvenient, we still need to speak the Lord to people, to testify for the Lord. If we would do this, spontaneously we will live an overcoming life. The first two items are concerning ourselves that we may be equipped. The following items are the living we ought to have for our serving the Lord.

SERVING THE LORD AND PERFECTING OTHERS

Third, we must gain people by preaching the gospel. It does not matter who we are, we need to preach the gospel. To preach the gospel is our heavenly profession. We do this by visiting people twice a month for two hours each time. If all the brothers and sisters here are willing to do this, formed in teams of three, working with each other, going to preach the gospel by visiting people twice a month, then you can bring in at least one person per month. That will be twelve persons in a year. As an average, every person can gain four new ones a year.

Fourth, we must perfect the new believers. After we have baptized a new believer, we should not leave right away, but stay for half an hour to an hour to start immediately to set up a meeting in his home (Acts 2:46; 5:42). After that, we go there every few days, and then once a week. We have to lead him this way for about a year. We lead the new believers to go on in the spiritual life and to function in the meetings. We have to teach them how to speak, pray, call hymns, and speak the Lord in the meetings.

Fifth, we must lead a small number of believers by setting up group meetings. Not only do we need to go to the saints' homes to have meetings, but we need to also lead the new believers to gradually get connected with the neighboring saints, by setting up group meetings that they can have fellowship and contact with one another. In this way they will be stabilized. Then, we lead the new believers to go on further in functioning in the group meetings by speaking for the Lord.

Sixth, we must participate in the district meetings. Finally, we also need to bring the new believers to the district meetings to help them do their best to speak for the Lord and speak forth the Lord (1 Cor. 14:26, 31). In the meetings, if anyone has a hymn, or a teaching, or a revelation, they may pour forth their portion, because we all can prophesy for the Lord one by one. We exercise to be in the same flow and to coordinate with the saints in speaking for the Lord, and we supply to perfect the saints, building up the Body of Christ (Eph. 4:12).

A LIVING FULL OF THE BLESSING

For this kind of living, the working saints should arrange their time every week properly. Every week I need to lead a home meeting and also to help out a group meeting, and then attend the Lord's Day district meeting, plus the Tuesday prayer and service meeting. Besides this, I would go out to preach the gospel by visiting people every other week. If we would properly arrange our time, I definitely believe that doing this should be very easy. However, in order to be able to do this continuously throughout the year according to a schedule and a plan is not an easy thing. Therefore we need a kind of miraculous life and power, that is our Lord Jesus, to supply us inwardly so that we can live this kind of normal Christian life.

May we all rise up to cooperate with the Lord to receive the burden to push this matter that we may do this continuously. If there is a place with one hundred people meeting together, and forty or fifty of them are willing to practice this—going to gain people by preaching the gospel, perfecting the new believers, leading the group meetings, and attending the district meetings—then assuming that one person can bring in two new ones per year, there will be a one hundred percent increase rate. Even if they can only bring one half of that, they will still get a fifty percent increase; this is for sure. As long as everyone is willing to do this, this is a highway to us. This matter all depends on the brothers and sisters living this kind of miraculous yet normal living every day—going out, coming in, going to work, doing business, and staying at home at proper times, doing everything according to schedule in a regulated way, being revived every morning, and living an overcoming life every day. In this way, not only can we ourselves be preserved, but also it will be beneficial to others. We ourselves can have such an enjoyable church life, our Lord will get the glory, and everyone can be blessed.

(Spoken by Brother Witness Lee on April 17, 1988 in Taipei)

CHAPTER FIVE

THE FATHER'S STRENGTHENING AND CHRIST'S MAKING HOME

Scripture Reading: Eph. 3:14-21

OUTLINE

I. The Father's strengthening—v. 16:
   A. According to the riches of His glory.
   B. Through His Spirit.
   C. With power.
   D. To be strengthened into the inner man.
II. Christ's making His home—vv. 17-19:
   A. Through faith.
   B. In our hearts.
   C. Rooted and grounded in love.
   D. Strong to apprehend with all the saints the breadth and length and height and depth.
   E. To know the knowledge-surpassing love of Christ.
   F. That we may be filled by the Triune God unto all the fullness (expression) of God.
III. The apostle's conviction—vv. 20-21:
   A. God is able.
   B. According to the power which operates in us.
   C. To do superabundantly.
   D. Above all that we ask or think.
   E. To God be the glory in the church and in Christ Jesus unto all the generations of the age of the ages. Amen.

A PROFOUND AND HIGH PRAYER

The passage that we have read is the second of the two important prayers of the Apostle Paul in the book of Ephesians.

In the first prayer, Paul prayed for revelation for the saints that they might see the hope of God's calling, the riches of the glory of His inheritance in the saints, the power of God toward us, and the church which God is after, which is the Body, the fullness of Christ (1:15-23). In the second prayer, Paul prayed for experience for the saints. This prayer has turned from the objective aspect to the subjective aspect. It can be considered the most profound and the highest prayer in the Bible. There never was, and there probably never will be, another prayer like this. In John 17 the Lord Jesus prayed to the Father. It was a very deep prayer. But Paul's prayer here is profound and high. One cannot find such a prayer in the Old Testament. In the New Testament, there is no other place that records a prayer as profound and high.

The focus of this prayer is that Christ, who is the embodiment of the Triune God, intends to make His home in the believers and to be deeply rooted in their hearts. Without Paul's prayer, even though we have the Gospel of John and the fourteen Epistles of Paul, plus Peter's writings and John's other writings, we would still be unable to realize that our relationship with Christ is so intimate, that Christ is to be our content, and that He desires to make His home in every part of our being, making us His habitation to express Him. When we speak of the church life, we must understand it to such an extent and enter into the reality in such a way.

We know that a dweller is the content of a dwelling. With the same house, different dwellers result in different contents. According to Paul's vision, we the believers are the dwelling of Christ. Our content is the all-inclusive Christ, who is the embodiment of the Triune God. He desires to make His home in us and to be deeply rooted in us.

The working saints are the core group in the church life today. I hope that you will all realize this. This will encourage and attract you. It will fill you with a firm conviction. Today in a city like Taipei, there are many attractions. It is easy for you to be affected. On the one hand, Christ desires to gain you. On the other hand, the world wants to occupy you. Are you going to go after the world? Or are you going to go after Christ? The choice is entirely up to you. But how you choose depends on your valuation of the object chosen. This is why I want to unveil to you the treasure that we have, so that you can have a comparison and will be able to make a choice.

In Luke 14 when the Lord Jesus taught the people the way to follow Him, He also mentioned the matters of reckoning and of considering the price. He used two illustrations, saying, "For which of you, wanting to build a tower, will not first sit down and calculate the cost, whether he has enough to complete it? Otherwise, when he has laid a foundation and is not able to finish, all those looking on will begin to mock him, saying, This man began to build and was not able to finish. Or what king, going to engage another king in war, will not first sit down and deliberate whether he is able with ten thousand to meet the one coming against him with twenty thousand? Otherwise, while he is yet at a distance, he will send an envoy and ask for the terms of peace" (vv. 28-32). The principle is the same in our following the Lord. There is the need for us to consecrate all we are and have in this life.

THE FATHER'S STRENGTHENING

If there were no God, no man could write a passage like Ephesians 3, because this chapter is too profound. It far exceeds the limit of man's imagination. This Triune God has passed through all kinds of processes—creation, incarnation, human living, crucifixion, resurrection, and ascension—to become the life-giving Spirit. Today, He is not only in us the believers, but He is also making His home in our hearts. As such, He is our life and content. This is why Paul said that Christ Jesus is the treasure within us (2 Cor. 4:7). Our knowledge of such a One is excellency itself (Phil. 3:8).

In order that the saints might see and experience this, Paul bowed his knees and prayed to the Father. The Father is the source of everything. Of Him every family in the heavens and on earth is named. Not only are we the regenerated believers of Him, but the whole created human race, the house of Israel, and even the angels are all of Him. The apostle prayed to such a Father that He would grant the believers, according to the riches of His glory, to be strengthened with power through His Spirit into the inner man. When I read this passage in my youth, I did not understand the meaning of being "strengthened with power...into the inner man." After a few decades, I was still not too clear. But gradually, during the last twenty years, due to my understanding of the Bible plus the spiritual experiences I have gained, I have come to realize this matter much more clearly.

In order to make you clear, I would put it this way. Man is of three parts. Outwardly there is the body, which is for contacting the physical world. Within there is the soul, with its self-consciousness; it is the seat of our personality. The deepest part is the spirit, with its God-consciousness. With the spirit we can contact God. Before we were saved, our spirit was dead and had lost its function. We lived by the body and the soul. Some are strong in their bodies. Others are strong in their souls. One day, we were saved. God forgave our sins, and His Spirit entered into our spirit, quickening us and enlivening our spirit. From then on, we were regenerated and now possess the life of God. However, our body and soul are not changed much. Those who are strong in their bodies remain strong in their bodies. Those who are strong in their souls remain strong in their souls. Most of the brothers are still strong in their mind. They like to argue. The sisters, on the other hand, are strong in their emotions; their hearts are more calculating and careful. Now we all are saved and are coming together to have the church life and the family life. Because our spirits are not strong enough, the brothers may still live habitually in the mind, and the sisters may still live habitually in the emotion. As a result, we produce conflicts and difficulties. For this reason, we need Paul's prayer, that the Father would grant us, according to the riches of His glory, to be strengthened with power through His Spirit into the inner man, which is our regenerated spirit.

When we are strengthened into the inner man, and when our spirits become strong, the sisters will be able to overcome their unstable emotions, and the brothers will be able to overcome their debating mind. In this way, when everyone turns to the spirit and allows the Lord to be the Lord, and when everyone walks by the Spirit, there will spontaneously be no conflicts or difficulties. In the family life, how can there be no arguments between the husband and the wife? The only way is through the strengthening into the inner man. When the spirit is so strong that it prevails over the emotion and the mind, no argument can go on. Otherwise, the more one talks, the more reasonings there are; the more one argues, the more there is to argue about; and the more two people argue with each other, the more their souls are strengthened. In the same way, in the church life, we need to have a strong spirit. How can we be without murmuring and striving? How can we be without criticisms and judgments? How can there be no rights or wrongs? Only by a strong spirit can all these be removed. The strongest part of our being should be our spirit. It should be stronger than our soul and should control our mind, emotion, and will. Only then will we have a proper, healthy Christian family life and church life.

CHRIST'S MAKING HIS HOME

When our spirit becomes strong and prevails over our soul, we are being strengthened into the inner man. Then Christ will be able to make His home in our hearts through faith. In the past, although Christ was in our spirit, our spirit was not strong. As a result, it was not the spirit which was the master. Rather, it was the soul which was the master, and Christ had no way to make His home in our hearts. Only when our spirit becomes strong and prevails over our soul are we able to give in to Him, thus giving Him the opportunity to make His home in our hearts. All the married brothers and sisters have this experience. Sometimes a couple will argue with each other. While the two are exchanging words with each other, Christ has no way to settle down within them. When He cannot make His home in your heart and has no way to move out of your spirit, He suffers greatly.

Some of you live in the brothers' houses or sisters' houses. Often a small matter will cause unhappiness among you. At the beginning when you live together, everything is sweet. It is like a honeymoon. But this wonderful situation does not last long. Gradually, the honeymoon goes away, and there begins to be an unhappy feeling among you. There is either incompatibility in disposition or difficulty in adjusting to different ways of living. For all these problems, no way will work. The only thing that works is to be strengthened into the inner man. When our spirit is strong to overcome the soul, Christ will have a chance to make His home in our hearts. Once He settles down and is at ease, you and I will also be at ease. When He is at peace, we are also at peace.

Being Rooted and Grounded in Love

Our heart is like a house with four rooms, which are the mind, the emotion, the will, and the conscience. When our spirit is strong and our inner man is being strengthened, every room in our heart is occupied by the Lord, and every part of our heart can be under the Lord's control. In this way, Christ will make His home in our heart, and we can be rooted and grounded in love. When we Christians are saved, a basic matter happens between God and us and between ourselves and the saints. It is a story of love, and this love is just God Himself. Because of our regeneration, we have the life of God and have become God's farm and God's building (1 Cor. 3:9). Since we are God's farm, we need to grow and be rooted. And since we are God's building, we need to be built up and be grounded. Both of these items, the rooting and the grounding, are all in love. For us to be rooted and grounded in the love of Christ is for us to grow and be built up in His life. The result is that we are strong to apprehend with all the saints what is the breadth and length and height and depth.

Breadth, length, height, and depth are all dimensions of Christ. These dimensions are unlimited in the universe. Everything about Christ is unlimited. His love is unlimited. His patience is unlimited. His humility, loving-kindness, goodness, etc. are all unlimited. All these are to be our practical experiences in the church life. This is not all. We are to know the knowledge-surpassing love. The words "to know" here mean to touch, taste, and experience. The love of Christ is just Christ Himself. Christ Himself is unlimited. So is His love. That is why we have the love that surpasses all knowledge. Yet we can know this knowledge-surpassing love through our experience.

Becoming the Fullness of God

When Christ makes His home in our hearts, and when we are strong to apprehend with all the saints the dimensions of Christ and to know the knowledge-surpassing love of Him through our experience, we will be filled by the Triune God with all His virtues and attributes to become the fullness of God expressing all His riches. This fullness is the church, the corporate expression of God for the fulfillment of His desire. This is too tremendous a matter. During the past sixty years, I have seen many among us who have given up golden opportunities of high positions and material riches to stay in the church life to live a normal and simple life. Through the operation of the Triune God, they have lived out in a practical way this portion of the word in Ephesians 3. The effect of this choice is too great. Only eternity can tell its worth. For this reason, I hope that you would all pay a high price to live such a church life.

Genesis 2 shows us that after God created man, He put man in the garden of Eden to enjoy the fruit of the tree of life and to dress and keep the garden (vv. 8-16). By then, God was everything to man. He was man's entertainment, satisfaction, and protection. But through the fall, man lost God and also lost everything else. After this, the descendants of Cain developed the harp and the organ, the keeping of cattle and farming, and all kinds of artificers of brass and iron (Gen. 4:16-22). They began to seek after pleasure, satisfaction, and security by themselves, and they put God aside. This is the condition of the whole world today. It has deserted God to seek for its own pleasure, satisfaction, and security. Among the nations, between individuals, in society and the homes, everyone is striving and fighting for these things. However, we are those who are saved by the Lord and called by God. We do not live for these things. Although we work and strive in society, our pleasure, satisfaction, and protection is God. When we enjoy God as our all, we will not come under the world's attraction and bondage, but will be able to fellowship with God in tranquility, living a normal and peaceful life. The result is that we will be able to live the real church life, experiencing Christ and expressing God's riches.

THE APOSTLE'S CONVICTION

At the end of this passage in Ephesians 3, we see the apostle's firm conviction in this matter. He was convinced that all his prayers would be fulfilled by God. He said that God is able to do superabundantly above all that he asked or thought according to the power which operates in the believers. This is Paul's conviction. It is also our conviction. Tonight, I present this word to you. I am convinced that ultimately God will fulfill these things among us, even beyond what we ask or think, that glory may be unto Him in the church and in Christ Jesus unto all the generations of the age of the ages. Amen.

For the church to arrive at this glorious stage, God needs a group of people on earth today who are separated from the world and are even separated from other Christians to be the pillars against the tide of the age. They are constantly being strengthened into the inner man to escape the corruption from the lusts. Their souls are fully under the control of the spirit. In their hearts Christ is making His home. Throughout the ages, countless saints have given up every worldly thing and have chosen to take this way as a result of seeing this vision. The Lord's testimony is able to continue today because practically, throughout the last two thousand years, there have been people who were willing to live this kind of life and have this kind of spirit. Today, without this kind of life and this kind of spirit, the new way is a vain theory. The life pulse of the new way is this kind of living and this kind of spirit. It is what Ephesians 3:14-21 is all about. Every one whose eyes are open will see the preciousness in these matters.

I have laid these matters before you. I hope that you will make a comparison and will make a wise choice. Everything depends on your discernment. It also depends on how much you are strengthened into the inner man. For our living, we have to follow the Lord's leading to fulfill our duty. For our future, we have to be strong in spirit to choose God's will.

Since God has spoken His word, surely He will fulfill His word. He is the Lord of the heavens and the earth. He will surely find a group of people who will accomplish His purpose. In this universe, this matter will surely see its ultimate consummation, which is the New Jerusalem, the testimony of God in eternity. Our church life today is a miniature of this testimony. May we give ourselves to this and be part of this glorious economy of the Triune God.

(A message given by Brother Witness Lee in Taipei on April 17, 1988)

CHAPTER SIX

THE RELATIONSHIP BETWEEN THE WORKING SAINTS AND THE NEW WAY IN THE LORD'S RECOVERY

Scripture Reading: 1 John 2:13-17; Phil. 1:19-21a; Eph. 4:12, 16; 2 Tim. 4:7-8, 18b

OUTLINE

I. God's need in His economy today:
   A. The young and the middle-aged saints—1 John 2:13-17:
      1. Those believers who are grown-up in God's life.
      2. Having overcome the evil one.
      3. Being strong.
      4. Having the word of God abiding within.
      5. Loving not the world nor the things of the world.
      6. Practicing the will of God.
   B. The saints who are the fathers—1 John 2:13-14:
      1. Those believers who are mature in God's life.
      2. Knowing the Christ who was before all things, who also is the Word of life who was there in the beginning—1 John 1:1.
      3. Continuing to know this eternal Christ by the inner life until maturity.
   C. The Lord's achievement in grace:
      1. In time and place.
      2. In circumstances.
      3. In grace.
      4. In the church.
II. In the past, there being many men and few opportunities, whereas now, there being many opportunities and few men:

A. The meetings and the service in the past not affording enough opportunity for the saints to serve:
  1. On the one hand, helping people to be regenerated and to grow.
  2. On the other hand, taking away peoples' opportunity to serve the Lord.
B. The meetings and the service today creating unlimited opportunities for the saints to serve:
  1. Opportunity abounding everywhere, from preaching the gospel by visitation, through the home meetings, to the small group meetings and the district meetings.
  2. Affording the saints the chance to let out a breath of life, which is their desire to serve the Lord.

III. Meeting the Lord's present need:
A. By recalling the past experiences and vision.
B. By responding to the Lord's attraction and calling.
C. By renewing the former commitment and consecration.
D. By setting aside one's time and specifically budgeting one's daily life.
E. By fulfilling all the needs in the new way:
  1. Visiting people to preach the gospel and to gain new ones.
  2. Regularly and consistently helping the new ones in the home meetings.
  3. Diligently learning to help the small group meetings.
  4. Seriously pursuing functioning and prophesying in the district meetings.

IV. A glorious living and a glorious goal:
A. Living—to live Christ—Phil. 1:19-21a.
B. Goal—to build up the Body of Christ—Eph. 4:12, 16.
C. Result—to receive the reward in the kingdom—2 Tim. 4:7-8, 18b.

In this training for the working saints, I have a heavy burden. There are many things I want to say to you. Tonight, we want to consider the relationship between the working saints and the new way in the Lord's recovery. Recently, I heard a saying that the working saints are the backbone of the church. I feel that this description is most appropriate. The working saints are the backbone of the church. When a man has trouble with his backbone, his whole body is in trouble. The older folks are especially careful to protect their backbones. The backbone is a very important part of a man's body. In the same way, the working saints are very important in the new way in the Lord's recovery.

GOD'S NEED IN HIS ECONOMY TODAY

The Young and the Middle-aged Saints

God's economy is to dispense Himself into His created and chosen people that they may be regenerated to become His children and the members of Christ through transformation, conformation, and eventually glorification. When these ones come together, they constitute the Body of Christ to express the Triune God in eternity. Strictly speaking, the Lord's recovery is simply God's economy. This new way in the recovery is simply a way to practice God's economy. Hence, the new way is not merely a matter of preaching the gospel and bringing sinners to believe in the Lord and be saved. That is only the initial stage. The new way is to carry out God's economy all the way from God's dispensing to His expression.

This way is a way of labor, striving, and struggle. I myself deeply feel that my experience during the past three and a half years has been one of laboring and striving. It is not a simple matter to bring a large church like the church in Taipei to the proper track of the new way. But tonight from the depths of my heart I do thank God for His grace. We should all bow down our heads and worship Him. The church in Taipei is now on the right track. The attendance at tonight's meeting is a proof that we are all on the right track.

What we need in the Lord's recovery now are the young and the middle-aged saints.

Those Believers Who Are Grown-up in God's Life

The first qualification of being a "young or middle-aged saint" is to grow up in the life of God. After three and a half years of experimenting, we have found out that after a person is baptized, we need to spend at least five to six months to feed him before he can become stable and somewhat free from the infant stage. You who are sitting here tonight have to admit that you have grown up in the life of God. How much more we should grow is a different question; but nevertheless, you have all grown.

Overcoming the Evil One

The evil one means something pernicious, harmfully evil, affecting and influencing others to be evil and vicious; it is personified. This personified one is Satan, the Devil, in whom the whole world lies (1 John 5:19). To overcome the evil one is a characteristic of a grown-up and strong saint (1 John 2:13b). He is nourished, strengthened, and maintained by the word of God. This word abides and operates in him to oppose Satan, the world, and all the lusts thereof.

Being Strong

The third qualification of being a young or middle-aged saint is to be strong (1 John 2:14b). Because these saints are strong, they can overcome the evil one.

Having the Word of God Abiding Within

The saints are strong because the word of God is abiding in them (1 John 2:14b). When a man has an empty stomach and is hungry, he will surely be weak; there is no possibility that he will be strong. But if he eats, his strength will return, and he will be strong. For you to be strong today, you need to be fed with the word of God. Without the word of God, it is impossible for a person to be strong.

THE WORKING SAINTS AND THE NEW WAY

Loving Not the World or the Things in the World

In order to occupy man, Satan uses religion, culture, commerce, entertainment, and other things to put man under a system. These things become a world system that is opposed to God. This whole satanic system lies in the evil one. Not loving the world is the ground to overcome the evil one. If we love the world a little, we will give ground for the evil one to defeat us and capture us (1 John 2:15).

Practicing the Will of God

Not only do we have to reject the world and the things in the world on the negative side, but, on the positive side, we have to practice the will of God (1 John 2:17). We are not practicing the will of God like someone practicing law. To us, the will of God should be a great thing that we practice all the time. In order for us to practice the will of God today, we have to practice the new way.

The Saints Who Are the Fathers

The present need in God's economy is not only of the young and the middle-aged saints, but of the saints who are the fathers as well. In the church in Taipei, there are many young and middle-aged saints. There are also many saints who are the fathers.

Those Believers Who Are Mature in God's Life

The saints who are the fathers are those who are mature in life. They are the ones who have known Him who is from the beginning (1 John 2:13). He who is from the beginning signifies the eternal Christ who was there before creation. The mark of a mature, experienced father is to know such an eternal Christ in the way of life. Christ is God. Only to say that He is God, however, does not convey our enjoyment of Him. We have to say that He is Christ. The word *Christ* signifies His being our Savior, His death on the cross for us, His resurrection, His becoming the life-giving Spirit, and His entering into us with all of His elements to become our enjoyment. What the fathers know is such an eternal Christ.

Knowing the Christ
Who Was before All Things,
Who Also Is the Word of Life
Who Was There in the Beginning

The saints who are the fathers know the Christ who was before all things, who also is the Word of life who was there in the beginning (1 John 2:13; 1:1). This Word was with God in eternity past before the foundation of the world; He also was God (John 1:1). In time, He became flesh. Life is in Him. This Word is the divine Person of Christ Himself. He is God's definition, explanation, and expression. Life is in Him, and He is even life itself.

Continuing to Know This Eternal Christ
by the Inner Life until Maturity

First John 2:13 says, "...fathers...have known Him who is from the beginning." The verb "have known" is in the present perfect tense. It indicates that the condition is continuing. The fathers have already known this enjoyable Christ by the inner life. Now they are continuing to know Him. This knowing is not once for all. Rather, it is a continuous knowing that reaches maturity.

The Lord's Achievement in Grace

Both the young and the middle-aged saints, as well as the saints who are the fathers, are what they are today because of the achievement of the Lord's grace. The Lord's gracious achievement is manifested in the time, the place, and the circumstances where we are. It is also manifested in the grace we have experienced and in the church life we have been put into. You can imagine that if you had not been born in this age and in this place, with the Lord's special provision in the environment, you might not have been saved. Our salvation is truly of the sovereignty of God. When I was young, I often worshipped the Lord for my salvation. He caused me to be born in the province of Shantung in China in the twentieth century. That was a place that the Western missionaries frequently visited. My mother was a third-generation Christian church member. I was even put into a Christian school. For every one of these points, I thank the Lord.

It is not uncommon for a person to be weak after he is saved. But in His recovery the Lord is especially gracious among us. The words released are rich, and the truth shines brightly. In addition, the church is like an orchard where life grows. The brothers and sisters are like fruit trees, growing day by day in this orchard. Some have been in this orchard from the time they were in the children's meeting. They have grown from being toddlers to become the elders serving in the church. Hence, in time, in place, in circumstance, in grace, and in the church, the grace of the Lord has nurtured and perfected us. Today, the church is full of young and middle-aged saints and has many fathers also. God's present need is for these two groups. If they are present, the new way will succeed. Without them, the new way will have problems. I do not say that it will fail, for God cannot fail. If He cannot get through in you, He will get through in someone else. Sooner or later, He will get through.

IN THE PAST, THERE BEING MANY MEN AND FEW OPPORTUNITIES, WHEREAS NOW, THERE BEING MANY OPPORTUNITIES AND FEW MEN

Three and a half years ago, there were those who wanted to serve in the church in Taipei, but the opportunities were few. Now the opportunities are too many. However, there are few who serve. At present, there are approximately ten thousand saints who monthly attend the home meetings, small group meetings, and district meetings. In addition to this group, there are about ten thousand dormant ones. Furthermore, since we began in 1986 preaching the gospel by knocking on doors, there are twenty-five thousand others who have not yet been brought in. If we add these dormant ones and the ones who have not yet been brought in, there are thirty-five thousand who need care. Who is going to care for them? In addition to the needs of these people, the home meetings, the small group meetings, the district meetings, and all the other meetings have their doors wide open.

The opportunities are there waiting. Hence, now there are many opportunities and few men.

The Present Meetings and Services Creating Unlimited Opportunities for the Saints to Serve

The meetings and services in the past did not create enough opportunities for the saints to serve. In the past, on the one hand, we brought people to be regenerated and to grow. On the other hand, we took away their opportunity to serve. Today, everywhere abounds with opportunity, from preaching the gospel by visitation, through the home meetings, to the small group meetings and the district meetings. At the same time, the Lord's grace is waiting there. If you do not know how to take care of a home meeting or a small group meeting, the church has the direction, and everyone can learn together. In the district meetings, everyone can prophesy, speaking the Lord's word and speaking for the Lord. Even if you say that you cannot do it, there is grace waiting for you to learn and to pick it up. Recently, many brothers and sisters who have been saved for only half a year have been standing up to prophesy in the meetings. The words they release are very fresh. This is a good sign. At present, opportunity to serve abounds everywhere.

The practice of the new way also affords the saints a chance to let out a breath of life, which is their desire to serve the Lord. When I was young, it was difficult to find an opportunity to serve. I attended worship services from my youth until I was twenty-six years old. During that time, no one ever asked me to pray, and I never dared to pray. When I was twenty-six, I attended a Bible study meeting. An older brother there who knew me realized that I loved the Lord. During one of the meetings, he called my name and asked me to offer a prayer. On the one hand, I was afraid. On the other hand, I felt privileged. Every one of us who is saved and loves the Lord has a desire to serve the Lord. There is a breath which we are ready to let out. Now the practice of the new way enables us to let out this breath of desire for serving the Lord.

MEETING THE LORD'S PRESENT NEED

In order to meet the Lord's present need, we must first recall our past experiences and vision. I believe all of you have had some experiences and some vision in the past. Now we have to recall them. Second, we have to respond to the Lord's attraction and calling. The fact that you are here today proves that the Lord has attracted you from within. In this attraction there is a calling that calls us to meet the need of the Lord in the new way today. Third, we have to renew our past commitment and consecration. In the past, many of us have had a heart for the Lord and have consecrated ourselves to the Lord. Now we need to have these renewed. Fourth, we need to set aside some time and specifically budget our lives. We have to set down some guidelines for our lives. In our daily lives, we should set aside some time for the service of the Lord. Fifth, we have to meet the different needs of the saints. There are the following four needs:

(1) Visit people to preach the gospel and to gain new ones. The practice of knocking on doors to visit people for the preaching of the gospel is absolutely correct. It should not be stopped. The only problem is that in the past few years we have knocked on too many doors and have saved too many people. We need a time of digestion.

(2) Regularly and consistently help the new ones in the home meetings. To help the new ones to have home meetings is a work that needs to be done regularly. We should visit them at least once a week.

(3) Diligently learn to help the small group meetings. All who have worked in the communities know that it is not easy to conduct a home meeting or a small group meeting. Especially the young saints, whose experience in the human life is not rich, find it hard to help others when family and marriage problems are involved. We have to learn all these things. For this purpose, the church also should give training of all kinds.

(4) Pursue seriously functioning and prophesying in the district meetings. This also requires a lot of learning. Now that we have the New Testament Recovery Version, it should help us somewhat in prophesying. For example, in the Chinese

Recovery Version there is a footnote to John 3:16 for the word "world." One day I came across this footnote and was very much impressed by it. This note describes man from his fall, with the poison of the serpent injected into him, until the New Jerusalem, where he becomes God's eternal expression. You should first study such a note at home and digest it a little. Then practice speaking it. In this way, you will be able to function and to prophesy when you come to the meetings.

Our life is to live Christ. Our goal is the building up of the Body of Christ. The result is the reward in the kingdom. This is the glorious life and the glorious goal for those saints who practice the new way.

(A message given by Brother Witness Lee in Taipei on May 22, 1988)

CHAPTER SEVEN

GIVE UP THE WORLD CHRIST TO OBTAIN

Scripture Reading: Heb. 11:24-27; Phil. 3:7-9a; 1 Cor. 9:17; Eph. 3:2; Col. 1:25; Eph. 2:20-22; 1 Cor. 3:10; 2 Tim. 4:7-8, 18a; 2 Cor. 12:15a; Luke 16:9; 1 Thes. 2:19-20; Matt. 25:21, 23; Eph. 4:11-16; 1 Tim. 3:15-16

OUTLINE

I. Examples in the Bible:
  A. The footsteps of Moses—Heb. 11:24-27:
    1. By faith refusing to be called the son of Pharaoh's daughter—v. 24.
    2. Choosing rather to be ill-treated with the people of God than to have the temporary enjoyment of sin—v. 25.
    3. Esteeming the reproach of the Christ greater riches than the treasures of Egypt—v. 26a.
    4. Looking away to the reward—v. 26b.
    5. By faith leaving Egypt—v. 27a.
    6. As seeing the invisible One—v. 27b.
  B. The image of Paul—Phil. 3:7-9a:
    1. Counting what things that were gains to him as loss on account of Christ—v. 7.
    2. Counting all things to be loss—v. 8a.
    3. On account of the excellency of the knowledge of Christ—v. 8b.
    4. Suffering the loss of all things and counting them refuse that he may gain Christ—v. 8c.
    5. Being found in Christ—v. 9a.
II. Rewards from gaining Christ:
  A. Moses:

1. Becoming the one to usher in the Old Testament ministry:
   a. Establishing the law—a testimony of God among men—Exo. 25:16.
   b. Building the tabernacle—a habitation of God among His people—Exo. 25:8-9.
2. Being qualified to enter the kingdom—Matt. 16:28—17:3; Heb. 11:26b.

B. Paul:
1. Becoming the one to usher in the New Testament ministry—1 Cor. 9:17; Eph. 3:2.
   a. Completing the word of God—the revelation of God's New Testament economy—Col. 1:25.
   b. Building up the Body of Christ—the habitation of God in the universe—Eph. 2:20-22; 1 Cor. 3:10.
2. Receiving the kingdom—2 Tim. 4:7-8, 18a.

III. The coming joy that results from being spent for Christ—2 Cor. 12:15a:
A. Being welcomed into the eternal tabernacles by those who receive benefit from you—Luke 16:9.
B. Having the ones that have received your help as your crown and joy at the coming of Christ—1 Thes. 2:19-20.
C. Participating in the joy of Christ in the kingdom—Matt. 25:21, 23.

IV. Completing the New Testament ministry—Eph. 4:11-12:
A. Building the church of God—1 Tim. 3:15-16.
   1. As the pillar and base of the truth—v. 15.
   2. As God's manifestation in the flesh—v. 16.
B. For the building up of the Body of Christ—Eph. 4:12-16.
   1. Arriving at the oneness in practicality— v 13a.
   2. Arriving at a full-grown man—v. 13b.
   3. Arriving at the measure of the stature of the fullness of Christ—v. 13c.
   4. No longer babes—v. 14.

GIVE UP THE WORLD CHRIST TO OBTAIN 71

    5. Holding to truth in love, growing up into Him in all things, who is the Head, Christ—v. 15.
    6. Out from the Head all the Body, fitted and knit together through every joint of the supply, according to the operation in measure of each one part, causing the growth of the Body unto the building up of itself in love—v. 16.

Although there are only three meetings for this training for the working saints, I hope to release all the burden I have within me. In the last chapter, we saw that the working brothers and sisters are the backbone of the church life. They are extremely important. This time our subject is, "Give up the world, Christ to obtain." We should give up the world to obtain the Lord Jesus, who is the all-inclusive Christ.

EXAMPLES IN THE BIBLE

The Footsteps of Moses

By Faith Refusing to Be Called the Son of Pharaoh's Daughter

In the Bible there are two examples. One is Moses in the Old Testament; the other is Paul in the New Testament. Both were willing to give up the enticing, tempting, and entangling world to gain Christ. Soon after Moses was born, he was taken into the house of Pharaoh and became the son of Pharaoh's daughter, which means he was the heir to the Egyptian throne. However, because he knew God (who was the coming Christ in the New Testament and who at the same time was Jehovah in the Old Testament) he refused to be called the son of Pharaoh's daughter (Heb. 11:24). "Je-" in the word Jesus is a short form of Jehovah. Therefore, Jesus is Jehovah in the Old Testament, and Jehovah in the Old Testament is Jesus in the New. The suffix "-sus" in the word Jesus means Savior. Hence, the name Jesus means Jehovah as Savior. The one who appeared to Moses was this Jehovah-Savior (Exo. 3:15). As far as the world was concerned, it was a rare opportunity to enter into the palace and be a prince. This could be considered as the highest and most honorable place on earth. However, because Moses knew

Jehovah, who was simply Christ, he refused by faith to be called the son of Pharaoh's daughter.

Choosing Rather to Be Ill-treated with the People of God Than to Have the Temporary Enjoyment of Sin

Moses chose rather to be ill-treated with the people of God than to have the temporary enjoyment of sin (Heb. 11:25). This signifies the enjoyment of Egypt, which is the enjoyment of the world and is sin in the eyes of God. The world is joined to sin. Sin occupies a great part of the world, and sinful things are also joined to the enjoyment of the lusts and the flesh. However, these enjoyments are temporary and transient. Because Moses knew Christ, he was willing to be ill-treated with the people of God rather than to stay in Egypt to have the temporary enjoyment of sin.

Esteeming the Reproach of the Christ Greater Riches Than the Treasures of Egypt

Moses esteemed the reproach of the Christ greater riches than the treasures of Egypt (Heb. 11:26). He made an estimation and reckoned that no matter how noble and precious the treasures of this world are, they cannot be compared with Christ. The last stanza of *Hymns,* #473, says,

> Arise! the holy bargain strike—
> The fragment for the whole—
> All men and all events alike
> Must serve the ransomed soul.
> All things are yours when you are His,
> And He and you are one;
> A boundless life in Him there is,
> Whence doubt and fear are gone.

I hope all the working brothers and sisters would have an esteeming and would consider what is noble and what is base. I made such an esteeming sixty years ago. At that time, I was still young and was as one charging on a great and tall horse into the world, ready to make gains. It seemed as if the Lord just took one look at me, and I fell from my horse. When I fell down, I began to reckon, "Should I choose the world, or should I choose Christ?" In the end, I was very clear that Christ is the best. From that day on, I chose to have Christ.

Looking Away to the Reward

After Moses chose Christ, he began to have a hope, which was to receive a reward from Him. Because of this, he looked away to this reward (Heb. 11:26b). This is not merely a reward for this life, but one that is for the life to come.

By Faith Leaving Egypt

Not only did Moses refuse to be called the son of Pharaoh's daughter through faith, but he also left Egypt by faith (Heb. 11:27). This means he left the world signified by Egypt.

As Seeing the Invisible One

By faith Moses "left Egypt, not fearing the wrath of the king, for he was steadfast as seeing the invisible One" (Heb. 11:27). He saw a vision there, and he was strengthened in his faith. In that vision, it was as if he had seen the invisible Lord. He met the Lord, and the Lord was seen by him. This is a tremendous thing. I hope that all the brothers and sisters, whether old or young, could say that they have seen the Lord. Although the Lord is invisible, I have definitely touched Him. This is why I know the way I am taking, and I know the kind of future which is ahead of me. These are the footsteps of Moses.

The Image of Paul

Counting What Things That Were Gains to Him As Loss on account of Christ

In the New Testament we have the image of Paul. The word image signifies a character and a model. Paul was a model of one who gives up the world to obtain Christ. Paul had a lot that he could boast of. He could boast of his birth, education, upbringing, and his ambitions and goals. One day on the way to Damascus, the Lord's light shone on him, and he fell to the ground. A voice said to him, "Saul, Saul, why are you persecuting Me?" (Acts 9:4). From that time on, his eyes were opened. He also had a reckoning. He reckoned "that the sufferings of this present time are not worthy to be compared with the coming glory to be revealed to us" (Rom. 8:18).

In Philippians 3:7 he said, "But what things were gains to me, these I have counted loss on account of Christ." The words "gains" and "loss" are both terms used in gambling. He counted all things that were gains to him now as loss because all those things which were gains to him result in the loss of Christ.

Counting All Things to Be Loss

Not only did Paul reckon as loss his Hebrew heritage, his Greek education, and his ambitions and goals, but he even counted all things to be loss (Phil. 3:8a).

On Account of the Excellency of the Knowledge of Christ

Paul counted it excellency to have the knowledge of Christ (Phil. 3:8b). This excellency does not refer only to Christ, but also to the knowledge of Christ. Paul considered it a matter of excellency to have more knowledge of Christ. The Jews considered the law given by God through Moses as the highest treasure in human history. This is why they were so zealous for the law. Formerly, Paul was such a person. But when God revealed Christ in him (Gal. 1:15-16), he saw a preciousness, an excellency, an unparalleled worth, and an extraordinary value that far transcended the law. Because of such a knowledge of Christ, he was able to count it a matter of excellency to have the knowledge of Christ.

Suffering the Loss of All Things, Counting Them Refuse for the Gaining of Christ

Paul said, "I have suffered the loss of all things and count them refuse that I may gain Christ" (Phil. 3:8b). Here Paul used the words "loss" and "gain" again. To the outsiders the way that he chose was a gambling. It was risky and could be dangerous. He had a very good background, he had received a high education and enviable positions, and he had a bright future. But he gave all these up for another choice. Was this not a dangerous gamble in the eyes of his contemporaries? But to Paul this was not dangerous because he knew God and His word. He knew what he was doing.

The reason I am speaking this message to the working brothers and sisters is that they are standing at the edge of a cliff. On the one side is Christ, and on the other side is the world. You can step over to the side of the world and fall, or you can step to the side of Christ and be lifted up. Today I have a burden to save your life. This is an eleventh-hour decision. You must not make the wrong choice. I am most thankful that on the afternoon I was saved in 1925, I made a right choice. I chose to have Christ and to reject the world! I have not regretted even until today. I believe I will never regret this choice.

Many brothers and sisters among you are very clear within they have to love the Lord and to stand on His side. But I am not sure about your condition. It seems that you are standing on the Lord's side. Yet you have left a bridge that links you to the world. You have not removed the bridge, much less burned it down, after you crossed the river. Abraham our forefather went to Canaan from Ur of the Chaldees. When he became weak, however, he did not return to Ur but went down to Egypt. Egypt is a place that is easy to return to. This message is my warning. Today, not only have I burned the bridge, but I have even lost my way of return. But you are all young and ambitious, or at least middle-aged and ambitious. What then shall you do? My burden this time is to infuse grace into you, that hopefully through the grace of the Lord your problems could be solved once for all and that you could say to the Lord, "Lord, burn my bridge! I cannot burn it, but please burn it for me." I hope that when you go home tonight, you would all have a bridge-burning prayer.

Being Found in Christ

Not only did Paul suffer the loss of all things and count them refuse, but he pursued to be found in Christ (Phil. 3:9). He desired to be seen by others as a man in Christ. In all things, great or small, and especially in his daily living, he was seen by others to be a man in Christ. When we love the world and pursue after it, others will surely not recognize us as Christians, because our goals, inclinations, and tastes are all worldly. Christ is not manifested that much in us. Paul desired earnestly for Christ to be manifested in him. Not only was he free from sin and the world, but he was full of Christ. This was what he was pursuing after.

REWARDS FROM GAINING CHRIST

The rewards received from gaining Christ are twofold. One is in this life, to be gained while one is alive on earth. The other is in the coming life, to be gained in the kingdom when the Lord comes back.

Moses—Becoming the One to Usher in the Old Testament Ministry

Establishing the Law— a Testimony of God among Men

Moses was made a person to usher in the Old Testament ministry. Although Abraham was noble, he did not bring in the Old Testament ministry. What is the Old Testament ministry? First, it is the establishing of the law. Today, we are too familiar with grace and have therefore overlooked the law and have even despised the value of the law. Actually, the law is not only the Ten Commandments with their many regulations and ordinances for man to keep; the law is a description depicting the nature of God. Before Moses brought in the law, not one patriarch could describe God in a way that could compare with the way the law did. In God's laws, especially in the Ten Commandments, God's characteristics are fully depicted. The Ten Commandments depicted God as the One who is love, light, holiness, and righteousness. Today, the whole world bases its laws on the Roman law. But the Roman law has as its basis the Ten Commandments of Moses. Hence, the reward of Moses was a tremendous one. He was the one who brought in the Old Testament ministry.

The first thing this ministry did was to bring the law of God to man, as a testimony of God among men.

Building the Tabernacle—
a Habitation of God among His People

The second item in the Old Testament ministry was the building up of the tabernacle. None of the patriarchs, including Enoch, Noah, Abraham, Isaac, and Jacob, brought God's habitation to earth. It was Moses who built a habitation for God on earth among the Israelites, making it possible for God to dwell with His people. This was the second great reward which Moses obtained in this world.

Moses—
Being Qualified to Enter the Kingdom

Moses may have been the first one to enter into the kingdom. The Lord said in Matthew 16:28: "There are some of those standing here who shall by no means taste death until they see the Son of Man coming in His kingdom." After six days, the Lord took Peter, James, and John to a high mountain, and He was transfigured before their eyes. There He unveiled His glory. Moses and Elijah were also there conversing with Him. This was a miniature of the millennial kingdom. There was the law represented by Moses. Hence, Moses took the lead to enter into the kingdom.

Paul—Becoming the One
to Usher in the New Testament Ministry

Completing the Word of God—
the Revelation of God's New Testament Economy

In principle, Paul was a person more or less the same as Moses. He brought in the New Testament ministry and completed the word of God. In Colossians 1:25 he said, "I became a minister according to the stewardship of God, which was given to me for you, to complete the word of God." To complete the word of God is to complete God's revelation. This revelation centers mainly on two things: the mystery of God, which is Christ, and the mystery of Christ, which is the church. On these two points, Paul completed the word of God and revealed to us God's economy in a full way.

Building Up the Body of Christ— the Habitation of God in the Universe

Moses' building of the Tabernacle was a type. In the New Testament, the Apostle Paul's building up of the Body of Christ was a reality.

Paul—Receiving the Kingdom

In 2 Timothy 4:18 Paul said, "The Lord will deliver me from every evil work, and will save me unto His heavenly kingdom." Hence, Paul was also able to enter into the kingdom. Please remember that when he spoke this word, he was being rejected by all the churches in Asia. Nevertheless, he knew that though he was rejected by earthly men, God would save him into His kingdom, because he had given up the world to gain Christ.

THE COMING JOY RESULTING FROM BEING SPENT FOR CHRIST

Second Corinthians 12:15 says, "But I will most gladly spend and be utterly spent on behalf of your souls." It is worthwhile for us to spend and be utterly spent for Christ. Paul said that he would most gladly spend for the saints not only his money, but himself. He spent both his money and himself for the Body of Christ. He put out all his money, time, energy, and even his own life. His labor for the saints was such that it was unto death. Today we should not keep our money in our own hands. Rather, we should give it away for Christ's sake. Not only do we have to give our money, but we have to give ourselves as well.

Being Welcomed into the Eternal Tabernacles by Those Who Receive Help from You

In Luke 16:9 the Lord said, "Make friends for yourselves by means of the mammon of unrighteousness, that when it fails, they may receive you into the eternal tabernacles." Mammon belongs to Satan's world. It is unrighteous in position and in existence. When the Satanic world passes away, mammon will become useless in the kingdom of God. For this reason, we have to seize the opportunity today to make friends by means of our mammon, which is to spend our money to preach the gospel and to bring sinners to salvation. When the Lord comes back, all those who have been saved by the gospel through your help will line up to welcome you into the eternal tabernacle. If you have never brought one to salvation, on that day others will have welcomers. But you will be all alone and will be put to shame. If we are busy day in and day out all day long here on earth, in the end what eternal value will there be to our labor? The only result that is everlasting is our sacrifice for the Lord in bringing others to salvation and helping them to be perfected.

Having the Ones Who Received Help as One's Crown and Joy at the Coming of Christ

When the Lord comes back, there will be those who line up to welcome Paul. There will also be those who are Paul's crown and joy. In 1 Thessalonians 2:19-20 Paul said, "For what is our hope or joy or crown of boasting? Are not even you, before our Lord Jesus at His coming? For you are our glory and joy." When the Lord comes back, those who have been saved through you will line up to welcome you. Those who have been edified, supplied, shepherded, and led by you will even be the crown on your head and will be your joy before the Lord and before the whole universe.

Participating in the Joy of Christ in the Kingdom

In Matthew 25, the Lord repeated twice the word about participating in the joy of Christ in the kingdom. The Lord said the same word to the good slave who gained five talents from five and to the one who gained two talents from two: "Well done, good and faithful slave; you were faithful over a few things, I will set you over many things; enter into the joy of your lord" (vv. 21, 23). The reason for their reward was that they cared for others, bringing them to salvation and gaining them for the Lord. When the Lord comes, they will be rewarded by participating in the joy of Christ in the kingdom.

COMPLETING THE NEW TESTAMENT MINISTRY
Building the Church of God
As the Pillar and Base of the Truth

These ones who have given up the world to gain Christ are working to complete the New Testament ministry. The work of the New Testament ministry is first the building up of the church of God. The church of God is the pillar and base of the truth in a locality. Truth here refers to the real things concerning Christ and the church according to God's New Testament economy. The church is the supporting pillar and holding base of all these realities. A local church today should hold, bear, and testify the truth of Christ and the church.

Those who are newly saved in the church have been saved recently out of the world; they do not know much about the truth. If you can speak some truth in the meeting, you will render them much help. The result is that the local church will become the pillar and base of the divine truth. Today we have the preaching of the gospel. We also have the home meetings, the small group meetings, and the district meetings. All these provide ample opportunity for you to minister the truth. If you would indeed give up the world to gain Christ and would take the burden of the building of the local church upon your shoulders, you have to learn the truth properly, grow in life, and speak the truth in the meetings. Not only should you speak the truth in the home meetings, the group meetings, and the district meetings; you need to speak the truth to your neighbors as well. The church is the pillar and base of the truth.

As God's Manifestation in the Flesh

When a local church becomes the pillar and base of the truth, it becomes God's manifestation in the flesh (1 Tim. 3:16). First Corinthians 14:24-25 says that when all speak for the Lord in the meeting, if an unbeliever comes, he will be convicted to say that God is really among us. If our meetings are in such a condition, they will be God manifested in the flesh. The function of the local churches is to support the truth of God. It is also to express God in the different localities.

For the Building Up of the Body of Christ
Arriving at the Practical Oneness

The building up of the Body of Christ is a very rich and profound subject. Due to the time, I can only point out a little bit. All six points in the outline are revelations from Ephesians 4:12-16. If the working saints can rise up, such a condition will be manifested in Taipei, that is, there will be a practical oneness seen. All the brothers and sisters will have no more opinions, because everyone will have grown in life. In a family, the most talkative ones are the young children. The same is true when a church is young. One would say something and another would say something else, and opinions are everywhere. By the gradual growth in life, everyone will arrive at the practical oneness—a oneness of the faith and of the full knowledge of the Son of God. By then, no one will need to say anything else. Everyone will be speaking about the faith and about Christ.

Arriving at a Full-grown Man

If the working saints will rise up today, the church will become a full-grown man. This is not a dream. A full-grown man is a mature man. This kind of maturity in life is necessary for the practical oneness.

Arriving at the Measure of the Stature of the Fullness of Christ

The fullness of Christ is His Body. This Body has a stature which has a measure. The arriving at the full-grown stature of the fullness of Christ is also a necessary step. Today in the church in Taipei, the measure of the stature of the Body of Christ cannot be considered as being full, because we have not yet arrived. That is why there is the need for the working ones to rise up.

No Longer Babes

At times some local churches are still in the stage of the babes. They are tossed to and fro by the different winds of teachings, doctrines, concepts, and opinions. But if the working saints would rise up, they will be delivered from the condition of the babes.

Holding to Truth in Love,
Growing Up into Him in All Things,
Who Is the Head, Christ

The meaning of holding to truth in love is to hold to Christ and His Body in the love of Christ, and not to be affected by the winds of teachings, nor to bring in elements foreign to the Body. To grow up into the Head in all things is to have Christ increase in us in all things until we become a full-grown man. Whether the church can arrive at this condition or not depends on the working brothers and sisters. Perhaps you would say that I am putting all the burden on your shoulders. That is right, because you are the backbone. The weight of the whole body is supported by the backbone.

Out from the Head
All the Body, Fitted and Knit Together
through Every Joint of the Supply,
according to the Operation
in Measure of Each One Part,
Causing the Growth of the Body
unto the Building Up of Itself in Love

First we grow into the Head. Then out from Him we have something for the building up of His Body. The Body of Christ grows by itself and is built up by itself, through every joint of the supply, which refers to the specially gifted ones, and the functioning parts, which refer to every member.

The reason we have to take the new way is that in the old way, it is very difficult for the brothers and sisters to be built up organically. A human body not only needs food, but needs exercise as well. The way in the past of one speaking and all the others listening was to give people food without giving them the organic exercise. Now for us to change to the new way means for us to let the children roll and jump. It may not be too orderly. But the organic capacity of every one will be realized. Hence, the present new way is to make every one a living person. You can realize that now there are unlimited needs. We need people to visit men and preach the gospel to them. We need people for the home meetings, the small group meetings, and the district meetings. Everywhere, there is the need for people to put in their share.

If all the working ones would rise up, some in the homes, some in the small group meetings, and some in the district meetings, with every one being a pillar and a core member, they will become fully useful, and the situation will be very glorious. Imagine how many people you will be built up with if, from the beginning of the year to the end, you bring in people every week and take care of them and supply them. I fully believe that these people will line up to welcome you in the future. Even today, they are already your crown and joy. For many of us, we have two kinds of children, the spiritual ones and the natural ones. Those who have the experience can testify that although we rejoice in seeing our natural children, we have more joy in seeing our spiritual children. Do not have as much consideration for your natural children. You have to consider a little your spiritual children before the Lord. Today the new way is somewhat laid out in Taipei. The framework is quite complete. The opportunities that have been generated are countless. The Lord brought us into this way in order to put all the opportunities before us. He is waiting for all to come. It will be glorious if you would become a part of it. It will be glorious not only when the Lord returns, but even right now today.

(A message given by Brother Witness Lee in Taipei on May 29, 1988)

CHAPTER EIGHT

A NORMAL LIFE AND SERVICE

Scripture Reading: Rom. 12:2; 2 Cor. 5:14-15; Acts 11:29; 1 Cor. 16:2; Rom. 12:1; 1:14; Matt. 4:19; 1 Tim. 2:1, 4; 1 Cor. 9:16-17; Acts 5:42; 1 Thes. 2:20; John 21:15-16; 4:24; Heb. 10:24-25; 1 Cor. 14:26, 1, 5, 39; Eph. 4:12, 15-16; Acts 6:7; 12:24; 19:20

OUTLINE

I. A normal life:
   A. Being different from the world—Rom. 12:2:
      1. Those in the world belong to the world and are for the world.
      2. The believers belong to the Lord and are for the Lord.
   B. Being constrained by the Lord to live to the Lord—2 Cor. 5:14-15.
   C. Setting up a schedule of one's daily life:
      1. One that is suitable for living to the Lord and serving Him.
      2. Having a budget in time, energy, and finances:
         a. Setting aside a fixed time every week and every day for the Lord.
         b. There being the need to budget one's strength for the Lord as well.
         c. In budgeting our finances, that which is for the Lord should be increased according to the prosperity bestowed by the Lord—Acts 11:29; 1 Cor. 16:2.

II. A normal service:
   A. Offering up our bodies and our time—Rom. 12:1:

1. According to budget.
2. Not owing the Lord—Rom. 1:14.
B. Preaching the gospel to gain new ones—Matt. 4:19:
 1. Being interested in sinners, and praying for the unbelievers—1 Tim. 2:1, 4.
 2. Not being something of a temporary zeal.
 3. But functioning in a normal and regular way—1 Cor. 9:16-17.
C. Taking care of the home meetings and perfecting the new ones—Acts 5:42:
 1. Considering the new ones as one's joy—1 Thes. 2:20.
 2. Teaching and shepherding patiently—John 21:15-16.
 3. Mainly cultivating the spirits of the new ones—John 4:24.
D. Helping the meetings and contacting the saints:
 1. Considering those being helped as one's glory.
 2. Helping them to mingle with the saints.
 3. Directing them to open to the saints for mutual fellowship, concern, love, and care—Heb. 10:24-25.
E. Attending the district meetings to build up the church:
 1. Before and after the meetings, contacting the new attendants and the other saints.
 2. Exercising to function in the meetings by testifying or prophesying—1 Cor. 14:1, 5, 39.
 3. Practice the voice and the proper use of time.
 4. Practice following the flow of the meeting and caring for others' feelings.
F. Building up the Body of Christ:
 1. By-passing arrangements, acting and serving organically.
 2. Not emphasizing work, but supplying Christ, life, and the Spirit.
 3. Leading others to learn to serve and work organically and to grow together with the

saints in the life of Christ, being fitted and knit together for the building up of the Body of Christ—Eph. 4:12, 15-16.
4. Boasting only in the work of gaining, perfecting, leading, and building up people.
5. That the all-inclusive Christ may have an unlimited and unceasing increase and spread—Acts 6:7; 12:24; 19:20.

Prayer: Lord, come and speak again tonight. Prove to us once more that You are one spirit with us. Speak in our speaking. Speak a clear word, a word of revelation. You and we are one spirit. This is not just a story of love, but a story of the spirit. Lord, we believe in Your presence. We believe that You are with us here in a rich way. Be gracious to us, and visit us. Touch the depths of our being, and speak to our depths. Grant us a new beginning, that we would learn to live a life of love and a life of being in the spirit. Lord! You should have the glory in us and should occupy the preeminent place in our lives. May we take this way all the days of our life. When we see You, may we be able to sing the song of victory. Amen.

A NORMAL LIFE
Different from the World

The subject today is a normal life and service. Basically speaking, we the Christians are different in our way of life from those in the world. They belong to the world and are for the world. We belong to the Lord and are for the Lord. Every lover of the Lord is, outwardly speaking, somewhat peculiar. Every day we have the Bible in our hands. We often go to the meeting halls. All the time we say "Hallelujah" and "Amen." In the morning we read the Bible. In the evening we read the same Bible. Sometimes we even have to read the Bible before going to bed. I advise those that have insomnia to make all necessary preparations for going to bed. Then, when they are ready to go to bed, I advise them to open up the Bible and read for ten minutes. After the reading, there is no need for too long a prayer. They may simply say, "Thank the Lord! Be with me, Lord! Amen," and then go to sleep. Many times, in this way, they will fall asleep right away. We Christians are uncommon because we belong to the Lord Jesus. We love Him and live for Him.

Living to the Lord
by the Constraining of His Love

The reason we are different from the others is that we have the love of the Lord in us. We are constrained by the Lord's love (2 Cor. 5:14). The word "constrain" is difficult to translate. Its original meaning is to be pressed on all sides, holding to one end, forcibly limited and confined to one object within certain bounds, being shut up to one line and purpose as in a narrow, walled road. Since the day you first belonged to the Lord, it seems as if the Lord has put two walls at your two sides. These two walls become a narrow lane that compels you to go forward. You cannot turn or take another way. You are compelled to take this way. By our nature, we do not want God. We only want ourselves. In our studying and working, it is always ourselves that is the center, the goal, and the perspective. But after we were saved, His love began to constrain us, and we began to love Him. When I was young, China was at the period of a great reform. I was educated mostly in the Western way. I had quite a bright future. How then did I end up being a "poor preacher"? It is because there is something that has constrained me to take the way of the Lord.

The Lord's love is too strong. He compels you to accept His love. The more you say that you would not love the Lord, the more He loves you. Wherever you go, the Lord follows you. He will not let you go until you respond to His love. The Lord's constraining is not mainly a constraining in environments. Rather, it is an inward constraining. It makes us uncomfortable when we do not love Him. All those who belong to the Lord and who love the Lord have been constrained to take this way. Our Lord indeed loves us. Nevertheless, I have never seen another person that bothers us as much as the Lord does. One brother testified that he asked for a leave of absence from the Lord to go to a movie. But the Lord would not let him go. He followed him. When he bought the ticket and entered the theater, the Lord followed him. Even during the most exciting moment, he could not shout. When he went home, he could not sleep the whole night long. In the end, he could not help but say to the Lord, "Lord! It is not that I love You. But You have bothered me too much, and there is nothing that I can do. I cannot go to the theater anymore." This is the meaning of constraining.

Once we submit to the Lord, He stops the constraining, and things become smooth. Formerly, I was all alone, by myself. The Lord was not there, and no one minded my business. Now the Lord is with me, and He minds my business. Thank the Lord! When our concept is changed this way, we will not feel that we are being constrained. The reason the Lord is constraining us this way is to turn us to live to Him (2 Cor. 5:15). The phrase "living to Him" is difficult to translate. It does not mean to live for the Lord. It means to live unto Him. The meaning of living to the Lord is deeper than to live for Him. To live for Him means that He and we are still two. But to live to Him means that we and the Lord are one. It is like a wife living to her husband in the marriage life. In such a way, we live a life of living to the Lord and being one with Him.

Setting Up a Proper Schedule
of One's Daily Life

You need to set up a proper schedule for your life. Formerly, you were not living to the Lord, and your way of living was like that of those in the world. But now you are living to the Lord; you should set up a new pattern of life. Speaking first of the small things of life, most people like to sleep a little late in the morning. This is especially true with the young people. But now, you have to get up at six-thirty in the morning. The first thing after getting up is to call "O Lord Jesus" and to pray. Speaking next of the more important things of life, most people want to seek after an academic degree and to be famous and glamorous in the world. Now that we love the Lord and live for Him, our way of living is changed. In everything we should still fulfill our duties properly. We study properly and work properly, without any special coveting. In an ordinary way, we should love the Lord and live for Him.

Formerly, our life was a struggle and a striving for success in the world. Now we live a simple life of loving the Lord, living for Him, raising a family, educating our children, and daily testifying and bringing people to Him. Even when we venture into business, we do so with a restraint. We only labor in a measured way. We would not be greedy, nor would we be lazy. Neither would we waste time. In this way, we will truly be a person that loves the Lord and lives for Him. Otherwise, even though you may have a strong desire, your outward way of living will eat you up totally and bind you. For this reason, our way of living has to be one that matches our desire to love Him, live for Him, and serve Him.

Having a Budget in Time, Energy, and Finances

We should have a budget for our time, our energy, and our finances. When people talk about budgeting, most of them consider only finances. But according to my experience, even our energy has to be budgeted. I know how much strength I have. Every day I can use only a certain amount of strength. Every time I have a cold, it is because I have overexerted myself. If I would control my time well, I would not have a cold. This is why I plan ahead how many messages I need to speak and how many people I need to see in a week. Although you are young, you should distribute your strength properly. In this way, you will be able to accomplish the proper tasks.

Timewise, every week and every day, we should set aside some time for the Lord. If you really love the Lord, at least you have to sanctify the Lord's Day for Him. The Lord's Day is the Lord's. In addition, you should devote at least one evening out of a week for helping others for the Lord's sake. Either you should go to preach the gospel to gain people, or you should go to others' homes to have home meetings or small group meetings with them. You do not have to do too much. If you would spend one evening a week, in a year there will be fifty-two evenings. If all the two thousand brothers and sisters sitting here would do this, many people can be cared for. Now we have thirty-eight thousand newly baptized ones.

Who is going to care for them? Although it is difficult to deliver a child, that is done in a day. It is more difficult to raise a child. It takes many years to raise a child. Hence, to bring people to salvation, then to bring them to a proper spiritual living, and to bring them to live the corporate church life as a testimony, requires a tremendous amount of manpower. If all of you here will labor and strive, the church in Taipei can very well become the most prosperous and thriving church on the whole earth.

In the world, the thing that worries the mothers the most is that their daughters would not know how to cook after they are married. But in the end, all the wives know how to cook. There are very few households that hire cooks. Spiritually speaking, to hire a pastor to preach in the meetings is to hire a cook. Today, in changing the system, we are saying that everyone has to cook. Recently, I have been very happy, because both locally and overseas there are reports that tell me that the new way is workable and that meetings in many places have become rich and high. Today, to practice the new way, everyone has to be diligent. The opportunities are there for everyone to take. We all have to live a revived and overcoming life.

Hence, the new way requires that everyone mean business the whole day long. In the morning we have to contact the Lord and read His Word. During the day we have to walk according to the Spirit. Every Lord's Day has to be sanctified, and every week we devote one evening for helping others. If we practice this now, when the Lord comes back we will then be able to give an account. Paul told us in 1 Corinthians 16 that if any man does not love the Lord, let him be accursed, and that the Lord will surely come and judge (vv. 22, 23). At my age today, I am still pleading with all of you. I surely have a burden. I have exhausted my all. I do this because I know that I will have to see my Lord and that I will be judged. I hope that you will also consider this matter seriously before the Lord.

In budgeting your finances, you should offer up what you have in excess according to the prosperity that the Lord has provided you (Acts 11:29; 1 Cor. 16:2). The word "prosper" in the original language means to advance well or to progress smoothly. It means to be successful and profitable in our business, career, or whatever else. To be prosperous is a gift from God which results in abundance and affluence. Take Taiwan as an example. It has turned from a place of perilous and poor conditions forty years ago to one with peaceful and rich conditions today. The foreigners have considered this to be a miracle. This is the Lord's work and His provision. Hence, this prosperity is from the Lord. We have to send out our riches and care for the poor according to the prosperity that the Lord has granted us. In budgeting our finances, we should increase our giving according to the prosperity provided by the Lord. For example, this year you may budget to give a tenth of what you have. Next year, you may have to adjust to twelve percent. By increasing this way, you will be blessed.

When I was young, I read a word by Benjamin Franklin. He said that it is easy to make money, but that it is hard to spend money. At that time, I could not understand this. Later I became clear. He was absolutely right. It is difficult to use the money that we earn in the right way. The money that you earn should firstly be used to honor the Lord. You should say to the Lord, "Lord, You have given me this. I am offering a tenth of this to you." As long as you have the heart, surely you can save one-tenth. You should save this money first, either for the preaching of the gospel, or to give to the poor. Only then will your money not be wasted. Only then will it be of value. But if you use your money on wasteful, luxurious, or lustful things, you will corrupt the society. Hence, the way of the Lord is a way of blessing. It is a blessing to you, to those that come into contact with you, and to society. If we want to follow the Lord, our financial planning for the Lord should be adjusted upward yearly.

A NORMAL SERVICE

Consecrating Our Bodies and Our Time

In order to have the proper service, we must first consecrate our bodies and our time. Romans chapter twelve shows us that to practice the Body life, we must first offer up our bodies. We have to say to the Lord, "Lord, my body is purchased by You. It is Your possession. I am consecrating it to You." To offer up the body, we have to offer up our time, because the body is in the time. If we cannot give our time, the body cannot be presented. Practically speaking, you should consecrate your body and your time according to the way of budgeting we described. Paul said in Romans 1:14 that he is a debtor to everyone. This is a debt to the Lord. If we do not preach the gospel and do not help others to go on, are we not indebted to the Lord? Hence, we have to consecrate our bodies and our time to preach the gospel and to help others. Only then will we not be indebted to the Lord.

Preaching the Gospel to Gain New Ones

The second item of a proper service is to preach the gospel to gain new ones. In order to preach the gospel, first we must be interested in sinners. We must not feel that they are evil or repulsive. If so, our gospel will not go out. Romans 5:8 says, "But God commends His own love to us in that while we were yet sinners Christ died for us." In Matthew 5:44 the Lord also said to love our enemies. Hence, we have to be interested in sinners. When others lie, you have to pity them. If they are saved, they will no longer lie. Man is corrupted by birth. If the Lord had not saved you, you would not be that much better than they are. Moreover, we have to pray for the unbelievers.

Our preaching of the gospel should not be with a temporary zeal. Many Christians become hot suddenly and also turn cold suddenly. This is not normal. We should serve in a normal and regular way. Once a week we go out to knock on doors to preach the gospel. First Corinthians 9:16 and 17 says, "For if I preach the gospel, I have nothing to boast of, for necessity is laid upon me; for woe to me if I do not preach the gospel. For if I do this voluntarily, I have a reward." It was Paul's commission to preach the gospel. If he would not preach, it would be a woe to him. We should see the same thing today.

Taking Care of the Home Meetings
and Perfecting the New Ones

After a person is baptized, he needs care, shepherding, feeding, and teaching. All these require our labor. During the last few years, we have baptized about thirty-eight thousand people through our door-knocking. All the brothers and sisters have to rise up and pick up the burden to care for them. This training is conducted with the hope that the working brothers and sisters would rise up to visit them week by week, caring for them in the home meetings, perfecting them there, and considering them as their joy (1 Thes. 2:20), teaching and shepherding them patiently (John 21:15-16), with the view mainly to develop their spirit (John 4:24). If everyone would practice this, the result will be very noticeable.

Attending the District Meetings
for the Building Up of the Church

The fifth point of our service is to attend the district meetings for the building up of the church (1 Cor. 14:26). Before and after the meetings, we should contact the new attendants and the other believers. I have noticed this lack among most brothers and sisters in the meetings. The reason for this is that no one has the habit of contacting people before and after meetings. We do not have to sit down that quickly before the meeting. We can wait at the door for the brothers and sisters to come. No matter who we see, we can spend a few minutes talking to them. After the meeting, we do not need to leave right away. Find someone to talk to. It is always beneficial for believers to contact each other. Spontaneously, there is the visitation, the shepherding, and the teaching. Next, we have to practice functioning in the meetings by testifying or prophesying. We must also practice our voice and our use of time. When we speak in public, we have to speak aloud. At the same time, the speaker should measure his time well. Three to five minutes is good enough. Do not speak too long. Lastly, learn to follow the flow of a meeting, and learn to take care of others' feeling. Every meeting has its flow. Do not talk about the north when others are talking about the south.

When you speak, you should care for the flow and for the feeling of others.

The Building Up of the Body of Christ

The last point in our service is the building up of the Body of Christ. This is very important. This matter cannot be realized in the meetings of Christianity. It can only be realized in the practice of the new way. In the new way, no one is monopolizing. Everyone has a chance. Nothing is according to arrangement. Everything is by the organic way and follows the leading of the spirit. For example, according to your plan, you may have every Friday set aside for going out. But this Monday, while you are praying and contacting the Lord, He may give you a leading to visit your cousin that very evening. This is to be organic. We should not have dead services that come from arrangements. Rather, we should have living services that come from being organic. We should bypass arrangements and serve and act organically. Christianity talks about organization and arrangements. But the new way requires that we serve organically. All the brothers and sisters should be led by the Lord daily. In this way, everyone will be built up organically. We will not be building up an organized congregation, but we will be building up the Body of Christ.

Moreover, we should not emphasize work, but should pay attention to supplying Christ, life, and the spirit. Most Christianity activities emphasize work. But we have to learn not to emphasize work. Rather we should emphasize the supplying of Christ, life, and the spirit. For example, a brother may come to fellowship with you. He may mention to you his family problems, that his wife is giving him a hard time. You should not exhort him to be patient, forbearing, or yielding. This is not Christ. You can share with him a testimony, or help him to read some verses. You may say something like this to him: "Brother, today, the Lord Jesus is in you. He is a living Lord, and He is with you all the time. You need to contact Him in the morning. When you see your wife losing her temper, you should begin to fellowship with the Lord within to receive His supply. We all need the filling of the

Spirit. We have no way to overcome our problems. But when the Spirit fills us, nothing else will matter anymore." When you fellowship with him this way, you are supplying Christ to him. You are also supplying the Spirit to him. By this, he will grow in life.

As a further step, in order to help others learn to serve and work in an organic way, we have to grow together with the saints in the life of Christ, being fitted and knit together to be built up into the Body of Christ. This is based upon the words of Ephesians chapter four. We are not merely coming together for a meeting or to build up a congregation, but are growing together into the Body of Christ. This is the building up of His Body. We should boast only in the gaining, perfecting, helping and building up of people. By this the all-inclusive Christ will have an unlimited and unceasing increase and spread.

(A message given by Brother Witness Lee in Taipei on June 5, 1988)

ABOUT THE AUTHOR

Witness Lee was born in 1905 in northern China and raised in a Christian family. At age 19 he was fully captured for Christ and immediately consecrated himself to preach the gospel for the rest of his life. Early in his service, he met Watchman Nee, a renowned preacher, teacher, and writer. Witness Lee labored together with Watchman Nee under his direction. In 1934 Watchman Nee entrusted Witness Lee with the responsibility for his publication operation, called the Shanghai Gospel Bookroom.

Prior to the Communist takeover in 1949, Witness Lee was sent by Watchman Nee and his other co-workers to Taiwan to ensure that the things delivered to them by the Lord would not be lost. Watchman Nee instructed Witness Lee to continue the former's publishing operation abroad as the Taiwan Gospel Bookroom, which has been publicly recognized as the publisher of Watchman Nee's works outside China. Witness Lee's work in Taiwan manifested the Lord's abundant blessing. From a mere 350 believers, newly fled from the mainland, the churches in Taiwan grew to 20,000 in five years.

In 1962 Witness Lee felt led of the Lord to come to the United States, settling in California. During his 35 years of service in the U.S., he ministered in weekly meetings and weekend conferences, delivering several thousand spoken messages. Much of his speaking has since been published as over 400 titles. Many of these have been translated into over fourteen languages. He gave his last public conference in February 1997 at the age of 91.

He leaves behind a prolific presentation of the truth in the Bible. His major work, *Life-study of the Bible,* comprises over 25,000 pages of commentary on every book of the Bible from the perspective of the believers' enjoyment and experience of God's divine life in Christ through the Holy Spirit. Witness Lee was the chief editor of a new translation of the New Testament into Chinese called the Recovery Version and directed the translation of the same into English. The Recovery Version also appears in a number of other languages. He provided an extensive body of footnotes, outlines, and spiritual cross references. A radio broadcast of his messages can be heard on Christian radio stations in the United States. In 1965 Witness Lee founded Living Stream Ministry, a non-profit corporation, located in Anaheim, California, which officially presents his and Watchman Nee's ministry.

Witness Lee's ministry emphasizes the experience of Christ as life and the practical oneness of the believers as the Body of Christ. Stressing the importance of attending to both these matters, he led the churches under his care to grow in Christian life and function. He was unbending in his conviction that God's goal is not narrow sectarianism but the Body of Christ. In time, believers began to meet simply as the church in their localities in response to this conviction. In recent years a number of new churches have been raised up in Russia and in many eastern European countries.

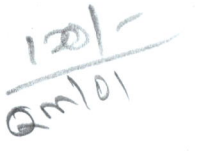

OTHER BOOKS PUBLISHED BY
Living Stream Ministry

Titles by Witness Lee:

Abraham—Called by God	978-0-7363-0359-0
The Experience of Life	978-0-87083-417-2
The Knowledge of Life	978-0-87083-419-6
The Tree of Life	978-0-87083-300-7
The Economy of God	978-0-87083-415-8
The Divine Economy	978-0-87083-268-0
God's New Testament Economy	978-0-87083-199-7
The World Situation and God's Move	978-0-87083-092-1
Christ vs. Religion	978-0-87083-010-5
The All-inclusive Christ	978-0-87083-020-4
Gospel Outlines	978-0-87083-039-6
Character	978-0-87083-322-9
The Secret of Experiencing Christ	978-0-87083-227-7
The Life and Way for the Practice of the Church Life	978-0-87083-785-2
The Basic Revelation in the Holy Scriptures	978-0-87083-105-8
The Crucial Revelation of Life in the Scriptures	978-0-87083-372-4
The Spirit with Our Spirit	978-0-87083-798-2
Christ as the Reality	978-0-87083-047-1
The Central Line of the Divine Revelation	978-0-87083-960-3
The Full Knowledge of the Word of God	978-0-87083-289-5
Watchman Nee—A Seer of the Divine Revelation ...	978-0-87083-625-1

Titles by Watchman Nee:

How to Study the Bible	978-0-7363-0407-8
God's Overcomers	978-0-7363-0433-7
The New Covenant	978-0-7363-0088-9
The Spiritual Man • 3 volumes	978-0-7363-0269-2
Authority and Submission	978-0-7363-0185-5
The Overcoming Life	978-1-57593-817-2
The Glorious Church	978-0-87083-745-6
The Prayer Ministry of the Church	978-0-87083-860-6
The Breaking of the Outer Man and the Release ...	978-1-57593-955-1
The Mystery of Christ	978-1-57593-954-4
The God of Abraham, Isaac, and Jacob	978-0-87083-932-0
The Song of Songs	978-0-87083-872-9
The Gospel of God • 2 volumes	978-1-57593-953-7
The Normal Christian Church Life	978-0-87083-027-3
The Character of the Lord's Worker	978-1-57593-322-1
The Normal Christian Faith	978-0-87083-748-7
Watchman Nee's Testimony	978-0-87083-051-8

Available at
Christian bookstores, or contact Living Stream Ministry
2431 W. La Palma Ave. • Anaheim, CA 92801
1-800-549-5164 • www.livingstream.com